PROGENY
AN ASTROLOGICAL RESEARCH

TIRUPUR S. GOPALAKRISHNAN

Translated by Sethumadhavan Venkatrao

ISBN   979-8-89415-004-8

Sree Uchishta Maha Ganapathy Namah!

Submitted at the Lotus feet of my Living God
Guruji Shri. S. Gopalakrishnan

Dedication

I offer my humble prayers

To

My Parents

Who have

Parented Me

And

Raised me up

Considering my development

As their own

Bless me Dad

Bless me Mom

PRAYER

Let us submit our prayers to

Our mother

Our Father

Those who were our preceptors and pedagogue till now by touching their lotus feet

Our family deity

Our tutelary God

Our chosen God

Guardian deity

Special/specific deities of the residential town

Let mystics, saints, gurus, spiritual heads, eminent astrologers, the five elements, nature, stellar constellation, the zodiac, the planets, and omnipresent power bless us.

Let our word, actions, and deeds not hurt or hinder people's progress.

Let peace prevail with all.

Sri Uchista Maha Ganapathaye Namah!

Sri Uchista Maha Ganapathaye Namah!

Sri Uchista Maha Ganapathaye Namah!

I always offer my prayers along the above lines at the start of every class.

I bestow this prayer to everybody.

PRAYERS TO PRECEPTOR

I hereby submit my humble prayers to
my father who is also my first preceptor in astrology
Late **Shri. N. Selvarasu Pillai for** giving me
love, education, pleasure, enlightenment, and knowledge
To my Guru Late Shri. Guru Ramasubbu
To my Guru who leads me in-absentia
Late Shri. K. S. Krishnamurthy (K.S.K)
I submit my humble prayers to all saints and spiritual
Gurus, Rishis, and the astrological fraternity.

My greetings to my fellow astrologers.

Seeking the blessings of all

Tirupur S. Gopalakrishnan (Tirupur GK)

SRI UCHISTA MAHA GANAPATHY NAMAH!

THANKS NOTE

This book was published in Tamil and received attention and appreciation from all.

I submit my humble thanks to my mentor and guide of all time Dr. K Nataraj PhD, (Astro), Oddanchathiram.

I take this opportunity to thank Guruji Shri L. Duraiswamy, Headmaster (Retd) and honorary President of Gurunathar Nadi Astrology Centre.

I would like to thank the Admin of GK Foundation Ms. Aswini K. Thangalakshmi - Sankarankoil for her efforts in the propagation of my astrological thoughts to all through our Foundation.

I also take this opportunity to express my sincere thanks to:

Mr. Sankar and Mrs. Tamizharasi , Tirupur

Mr. S. Balaji PhD (Astro), Srirangam

Sri D. Balakrishnan – Axe Oil, Chennai,

Sri R. Sakthivel – Ayyappa Label,

Sri P. R. Selvaganesh – Bangalore,

My well-wisher Sri Aditya Guruji – Chennai.

Mr. Sethumadhavan Venkatrao, Chennai for translating this book into English.

I must also thank

Sri S. Suresh – Coimbatore,

Sri B. Senthilkumar – Tirupur, all the GK Astro Admin-executives for their tireless support to me.

My sincere thanks to the management, executives, and staff of "Notion Press for bringing up this book in a fitting manner.

I convey my heartfelt thanks and blessings to everyone.

- Tirupur S. Gopalakrishnan, (Tirupur GK)

9842220903

Gkastro.tirupur@gmail.com

CONTENTS

ABOUT THE BOOK...

'The Clemency of Lord Shiva should reach all in its original form' is my motto. Sometimes Science wins over truth and wisdom, but it is the real truth and wisdom, clemency that wins over science. This has been proved many a time and childbirth is one such. Childbirth swaps between real truth and science giving astonishing results.

I have explained childbirth on more than 81 headers in easy ways to understand. These explanations are after research of more than hundreds of horoscopes/natal birth charts. The zero/nil/ill effect of thithis (distance between the Sun and the Moon – during waxing and waning), the explanation about malediction of Mars in scientific terms, Jeeva (soul) and Sareera (body) relativity theories, Beeja and Chethra (strength of sperm counts and childbearing capacity in women), planetary position in degrees that favour conception had been explained in depth and for easy understanding. I have omitted complex rules that can complicate results and given only those practical and simple rules to understand based on my experience.

The second edition of this book in Tamil finds more research additions and elaborations than the earlier one. I have attached a manual at the end of this book which throws light on a complete understanding of childbirth predictions to the users of this book.

With the blessings of Sri Ucchishta Maha Ganapathy

With the Grace of God and as His tool

Tirupur S. Gopalakrishnan

Mobile: 98422 20903

PROGENY AND ASTROLOGY

According to Saint Thiruvalluvar 'Children are called one's fortune'. Each of the nine planets is responsible for the respective month during the ten-month growth of the foetus's development. Their transit position is responsible for the finer growth or defective body parts depending on their benefic or malefic placements. A small compendium about the foetus's development.

10 MONTHLY DEVELOPMENT OF THE FETUS AND THE PLANETS

1. First month

   The male sperm penetrates the female egg or ovum in the female reproductive system for fertilization and Venus is responsible for this fertilization termed the zygote. And when Venus has been afflicted, the fertilization and the meeting of sperm and ovum (egg) are affected.

2. Mars is responsible for the transformation of the fertilized egg into a ball and afflicted Mars affects the irregular formation of the ball.

3. In the third month the ball moves into the form of an embryo with the formation of hands and legs abled by Jupiter. Any affliction to Jupiter at this stage affects the limbs that are growing.

4. During the fourth month the primitive face of the baby along with its throat, jaw, bones and nerves form, blood cells take a shape and the 'heart tube' starts beating. The Sun is responsible at this stage and any affliction to the Sun hinders this progress.

5. The Moon takes over the embryo's fifth-month development, supporting the growth of the tissues and tiny neural. An afflicted Moon hinders this formation and development.

6. The sixth month of the embryo is governed by Saturn which is responsible for the growth of hair, nails, and

body structure and any affliction to Saturn impacts the growth of the sixth-month embryo and related parts.

7. In the seventh-month development of the facial features, tiny buds grow fully and eventually into arms, fingers, toes, legs and eyes forming with movements of the body and breathing for which Mercury is responsible. Any affliction to Mercury at this stage affects the growth of respective parts.

8. In the eighth month, the embryo is called a fetus and it continues to mature and develop reserves of body fat, bain developing rapidly and the fetus can see and hear for which the ascendant lord is responsible. We designate the ascendant lord as the lord of life. Any affliction to the ascendant lord causes genetic diseases and poor immunity disrupting any antecedents to the eight-month fetus.

9. The Nine-month fetus continues to grow and the lungs are close to being fully developed with coordinated reflexes and can blink, close the eyes grasp firmly, and respond to sounds, light and touch for which the Moon is responsible. Hence, we term the Moon as the lord of the body. Any affliction to the Moon hinders the nine-month fetus and its body growth.

10. The grown-up fetus is ready to be born in the tenth month. We have seen a small hint about the planets responsible for the growth of each month of the fetus.

    Any afflicted planet becomes responsible for the defect in the parts of the body of its Karakathuva. In case of an eclipse after the formation of the embryo, the Karakathuva planetary parts of the body in which month the eclipse falls are affected.

    Suppose, the eclipse falls on the sixth month after the formation of the embryo, the planet responsible for the growth of the sixth month is Saturn and as Saturn is affected by the eclipse, the parts of the body denoted such as the hair, nails are affected and bones get broken. Detailed analysis and research of natal charts affected by eclipses on this basis will reveal so much minutest information.

PARTS OF THE BODY AND CONCERNED PLANETS

Part of the Body	Planet responsible for its formation
Head	Mars
Face	Venus
Neck	Mercury
Skin	Moon
Chest/Heart	Sun
Stomach	Jupiter
Thighs	Saturn
Bones	Rahu
Feet	Ketu

On the above lines, the Nine planets are responsible for the formation, growth and development of an embryo into a fetus and finally as a fully grown baby.

BHAVAGAS AND PROGENY

1st Bhavagam

The Physical strength of the body of a native can be known through this. If the ascendant lord is placed (hidden) in evil houses 6th, 8th, or 12th with malefic or the ascendant lord is combusted, then it will badly affect the body's strength during its Maha Dasha (Dasha) and Anthar Dasha (Bukthi).

If the ascendant lord is debilitated, the native will have a weak physique. Affliction with the ascendant lord will weaken the body of the native during his/her middle age.

Progeny will be delayed by retrograded ascendant lord and when disassociated with Rahu/Ketu.

2nd Bhavagam

This will indicate a new entrant to the family.

The presence of Rahu/Ketu in the 2nd bhavagam denotes the simultaneous repercussions of the increase in income but a decrease of love enjoyed or the addition of love/affection with a reduction in income.

The 2nd bhavagam indicates the new baby entrant who is born in a hospital or outside the house. Entry into the house should be strongly indicated by the 2nd bhavagam without which entry into the house is not possible.

The native will feel like an orphan in case of a weak 2nd bhavagam.

3rd Bhavagam

The 3rd Bhavaga will reveal the native's sexual desires, masculinity, femineity, potency, Capacity in satisfying the desires of the spouse or getting complete satisfaction from the spouse, the number of children that the native will have or has, their age difference, etc.,

4th Bhavagam

The 4th Bhavaga speaks about the disciplined behaviour of the native, the native's mother, the medical treatment of children, separation from children, comforts of the native, medical expenses of the children, and tough situations to decide whether to save the child or the mother during child delivery.

Separation of children and abortion (loss of a child) can be avoided if proper medical treatment is given during the 4th bhavaga Maha Dasa (Dasa), and Anthar Dasa (Bukthi). Powerful 4th bhavaga keeps the mother with potential strength but bothers the child.

For example,

A native has Sagittarius ascendant with Jupiter in Virgo. His mother surpassed too many crucial near-death situations and lives comfortably but got separated from the native.

Another native had Jupiter in Scorpio with Sagittarius ascendant and lived with his mother. He got separated from his children for 14 years who were studying in another state/ foreign nation.

5th Bhavaagam

Refers to Children, the five primordial elements, cosmic energy, (tutelary God), and Great Grandfather. UNASSOCIATED Rahu/Ketu with the fifth lord helps in getting good progeny and bringing them up well.

Combusted 5th lord blocks/forbids childbirth or denies happiness through children. Retrograde 5th lord delays childbirth.

6th Bhavagam

6th Bhavagam indicates the diseases that affect the native. Chronic diseases are indicated when Saturn/Rahu/Ketu and powerful inimical planets are associated/conjoined/aspect 6th Bhavagam.

The natives suffer from genetic disorders/inherit genetic diseases when Saturn is placed in the 6th Bhavaga or the 6th lord conjoins Saturn or Rahu/Ketu.

The Sun in 6th Bhavaga causes contagious diseases.

The association of the 5th lord with the 6th lord prevents childbirth due to diseases.

7th Bhavagam

7th Bhavagam always refers to the opposite sex/house. If 1st house is considered as a seed, then the 7th house can be construed as the earth/land. This house also refers to the 2nd child.

If both 1st and the 7th house are equally poised then it gives consistent/unobstructed/outright progeny and any defects/variance/defunct causes different results leading to a frustrated life.

8th Bhavagam

This Bhavagam refers to adopting a child or giving away a child for adoption. Greed-driven Gambling and Race after money is also referred to by this 8th Bhavaga.

If a native has Saturn or Mercury in his 8th Bhavaga with Jupiter's aspect on it, he will adopt a child but will face deadly events at the same time.

8th Bhavaga denotes the receipt of another's property or parting with own's property to others. During the treatment for test tube childbirth, if it happens to be the Maha Dasa (Dasa), Anthar Dasa (Bukthi) of the 8th Bhavaga, then the test tube baby is born through the sperm donated by another person.

When the 8th Bhavaga is connected or associated with the 5th Bhavaga, the progeny will be possible only with medical treatment. Hence it will be safe to adopt a child rather than go for medical treatment to have a child when the 5th and 8th Bhavaga is connected.

9th Bhavagam

This denotes the period of cure from diseases and that of the medical care a body is adapted to. It also indicates the responsiveness to medical treatment.

There will be no dissipation of money. A conjunction of connection between the 5th and 9th bhavagam will support better upbringing and wellness of the adopted child by the native. An attempt to inherit progeny as a test tube baby will be successful with great confidence.

10th Bhavagam

!0th Bhavaga refers to the past Karma of the native, separation from the family and insufficient time to care for the children.

11th Bhavagaam

This denotes the fulfilment of the desires of the native. (The time of fulfilment of the desire is based on the connectivity between the 3rd and 11th Bhavaga). To understand the fulfilment of a particular Bhavaga result, the 3rd and 11th Bhavaga connectivity of that Bhavaga should be reckoned.

The 11th Bhavaga supports the native to survive. (11th Bhavaga closely benefits the indicator of the native.)

Affliction to the 11th bhavaga denotes that the native is not doing good and remain unconscious at times.

12th Bhavagam

The 12th Bhavagam refers to the native's comforts and happiness. The native's fulfilment of sexual desires, contentment or distress can be known.

The presence of more than one malefic planet indicates long-duration hospitalisation or sufferings through chronic diseases.

The native's wealth, treasure, money or properties will be drained and enjoyed by others if malefic Rahu is present in the 12th Bhavagam

It is better if no planet is present in the 12th Bhavaga.

There will be excessive medical expenses when there is a planet in the 12th Bhavaga.

The Planet in the 12th Bhavaga will aspect 6th Bhavaga increasing medical expenses.

The 12th Bhavaga denotes contraceptive devices.

The 12th house defines retirement, relaxation, and longevity of the children.

Medical treatment and medicine consumption during the Maha Dasa (Dasa), and Anthar Dasa (Bukthi) period of the 12th Bhavaga for travel, sleep and sexual desire fulfilment will yield good results but cause a deficiency in sperm counts.

When retrograde planets are posited in the 12th Bhavagam in the natal (birth) chart, the medical expenses will increase when the same planet retrograde in transit.

THE BHAVAGA AND KARAKA INDICATORS OF CHILD BIRTH

The Bhavaga and Karaka responsible for childbirth are 5 and 11. Of these, the 5th Bhavaga for the husband will be the 11th for the wife and vice versa. Hence both the 5th and 11th Bhavaga are considered to be important in deciding the progeny of a couple. The Bhava lords of the 5th and 11th are responsible for showering the bliss of progeny.

For the child to be a recognised member of the family the 2nd Bhavaga is the main reason. To be precise as per the K.P. system, the 2nd, 5th, and 11th bhavagas are vital in deciding the progeny in a couple.

The planets posited in the 2nd, 5th, and 11th Bhavagas and the aspect of planets over these 2nd, 5th, and 11th Bhavagas should be reckoned in deciding the grant of progeny to a couple.

There is no classification as good and bad among planets. They do the job of the bhavagas in which they are posited and even if they are malefic in nature does give the bliss of a child when posited in the 2nd, 5th, and 11th houses. The Sun and Jupiter are the Karaka lords responsible for childbirth.

Jupiter is the Karaka lord for a Child.

The Sun is the Karaka lord as per Kalapurusha (Time personified) for a Child.

The Moon is the Karaka representing the uterus in women.

The 7th Bhavaga is responsible for the life forms in a child.

The 2nd, 5th, and 11th Bhavagas along with the planets posited in it, Jupiter, the Sun, and the Moon are responsible for giving progeny. According to my research, due weightage should be given to female horoscopes/natal (birth) charts rather than attaching importance to the male horoscopes/natal (birth) charts to see fruitful results.

Impotence can be seen only in males and not in females as successful artificial/IVF (In Vitro Fertilisation) otherwise known as test-tube babies proved this.

GENDER DISCRIMINATION

Based on Gender, the planets are classified. The planetary Karaka characteristics will be predominantly exhibited in the children born.

The Karaka planets influencing Male children:

The Sun, Jupiter, Mars, Rahu

The Karaka planets influencing female children:

Venus, and the Moon.

Neutral or Eunuch Planets:

Mercury, Saturn, Ketu. These three planets influence the birth of a higher number of female children or eunuch children.

Male, Female asterisms

Aswini, Punarvasu, Pushya (poosam), Hastham, Anuradha (Anusham), Sravana (Thiruvonam), Poorva Bhadra (Poorattathi), Uthra Bhadra (Uthirattathi) are the eight stars (asterisms) belonging to Male group.

Bharani, Krittika, Rohini, Ardira (Thiruvadhirai), Aslesha (Ayilyam), Makam, Purva Phalguni, Uthra Phalguni, Chitta (Chithirai), Swathi, Vishaka (Visakam), Jyeshta (Kettai), Poorvashada (Pooradam), Uthrashada (Uthiradam), Dhanishta (Avittam), Revathi are the thirteen stars (asterisms) that form a female group.

Mrigasira, Moola, and Sadhabisha (Sadayam) are considered neutral stars (asterisms). **Asterisms do not create genders but are responsible for determining the characters of gender discrimination.**

TROUBLE-MAKING SIGN IN PROGENY

Of the entire zodiac of twelve signs, the Scorpio sign is the maximum trouble-monger in extending malediction and sorrow/depression through children. The Scorpion sign and the planets posited in Scorpio are responsible for extending grief through children.

It is more to understand that the rest of the signs and planets posited in those signs are less harmful in extending malediction and sorrow through children.

Will there be a malediction between parents through children?

Male Children born in the birth asterisms/stars of their father and girl babies born in the asterisms/stars of their mother cause malediction by birth.

Definition

Such children born in the same asterisms/stars as their parents induce/trigger the existing malediction of their parents to undergo stress and strain. Newly born children never carry maledictions with them as they are considered angels/God. The existing malediction/curses/ill effects of the parents exhibited by the children's horoscopes are what I construe based on my research.

When parents do not suffer any maledictions, they need not fear and more importantly based on their children's horoscopes/natal (birth) chart.

If a girl baby is born in the asterism/star of her father, she brings fortune to her father and not a malediction.

Similarly, if a boy is born the asterism/star of his mother, he brings along good fortune to his mother rather than ill effects.

The above indicates the activation of good fortune by the children born.

MALEDICTION AND DISTRESS THROUGH CHILDREN

In the Parents' natal (birth) chart, there are two types of maledictions which are...

1. Malediction through Children

2. Distress through Children

Both these should be analysed separately.

Malediction through Children indicates either before childbirth or in having children.

Distress through Children can be after the birth of the Children, diseases to them or distress/pain through them or defects to the Children causing unbearable problems.

Distress in Children will take effect only after the experimentation of malediction through Children who should be discriminated against.

Certain planetary combinations will extend malediction only and not distress through children. Some other planetary combinations will cause only distress to children and not malediction through children.

These should be analysed well to arrive at clear results.

EFFECTS OF MALEDICTION/ DISTRESS THROUGH CHILDREN

Effects of Malediction on Children

1. Affliction of Progeny
2. Abortion after the formation of the fetus
3. Problems and diseases in sexual organs
4. Deficiency in sperm counts
5. Defective sperms
6. Lack of progeny even to healthy couples.
7. Pre-mature deliveries
8. Short-lived Children/Children with less longevity
9. Continuation of chronic diseases even after serious delivery
10. After getting descendants, situations make it impossible to nourish and maintain them.

Natal Charts with Malediction throughout Children may be classified into four types.

1. Remaining issueless for a few years after marriage.
2. Remaining childless even after so many years after marriage.
3. Childless couples.
4. Getting children after intensive medical treatment like IVF/sperm donors/surrogation etc., after a few years of marriage.

Distress through Children.

1. Children born with disability/defects/differently abled.

2. Children born with chronic diseases.

3. Children living alone and aloof from parents.

4. Death of children during the lifetime of parents.

5. Children born with gender disorders.

6. Children suffer more than their parents.

7. Children born without the capability to enjoy the fortune of their parents.

All the above Seven are the distress/sorrow felt by Parents through their Children.

For Example.

Emperor Dasharatha, the father of God SriRama suffered both malediction and distress through Children.

Emperor Dasharatha suffered a long time without Children and performed many fire rituals and homams. He got progeny but suffered a lot by separation from them.

HEINOUS, DEADLIER, AND EVIL INFLICTING HOUSES

For Movable ascendants, Planets posited in and lords of the 2nd, 7th, 8th, and 11th houses are severe trouble, mongers.

For Fixed ascendants, Planets posited in and lords of the 3rd, 8th, and 9th houses are severe trouble creators.

For Dual (Upaya) ascendants, Planets posited in and lords of the 7th, 8th, and 11th houses are severe trouble, mongers.

More than the lords of the Heinous, Deadlier, and Evil inflicting Houses, the planets posited in those houses are more vulnerable.

ZERO/CYPHER (VACUUM) (SOONYAM) THITHIS* AND CHILD BIRTH

*Thithis refers to the distance between the Sun and the Moon (Waxing and Waning Moon). Every day of the lunar transit is thithis

We have to look for cypher thithis before declaring the results. In childless couples, the cypher thithis have to be reckoned for evaluation of malediction and distress through children, useless relations, and parting away from family.

The Planet posited in the Zero/cypher(vacuum) thithis sign of the zodiac is ineffective.

The zero/cypher(vacuum) thithi signs and planets posited in those signs are mainly responsible for affecting the progeny.

Planets assigned to zero/cypher(vacuum) thithis or planets posited in the zero/cypher(vacuum) marked signs/Rasis of the zodiac will cause havoc in malediction or distress related to children matters during their Maha Dasa (Dasa), Anthar Dasa (Bukthi), and Prithyanthar Dasa (Anthra).

The zero/cypher(vacuum) thithis are classified into two:

1. Monthly zero effective thithis

2. Zero thithis

Of these two, the monthly zero effective thithis are based on the Sun in a sign at birth. That sign will be considered the monthly zero effective sign.

	Tamil Month	English Equivalent Period	Zero Effective Sign
1.	Chithirai	mid-April to mid-May	Aries (Mesha)
2.	Vaikasi	mid-May to mid-June	Taurus (Rishaba)
3.	Ani	mid-June to mid-July	Gemini (Mithuna)
4.	Adi	mid-July to mid-August	Cancer (Katakam)
5.	Avani	mid-August to mid-September	Leo (Simmam)
6.	Purattasi	mid-Suptember to mid-October	Virgo (Kanya)
7.	Iyppasi	mid-October to mid-November	Libra (Thulam)
8.	Karthigai	mid-November to mid-December	Scorpio (Viruchigam)
9.	Margazhi	mid-December to mid-January	Sagittarius (Dhanus)
10.	Thai	mid-January to mid-February	Capricorn (Makara)
11.	Masi	mid-February to mid-March	Aquarius (Kumbha)
12.	Panguni	mid-March to mid-April	Pisces (Meenam)

The above twelve are designated as Zero effective Months. More than the Zero effective month, **the thithis (Placement of the Moon from the Sun) is considered/termed more important. In the natal (birth) charts/horoscopes of childless couples, the Zero effective thithis plays a vital role**.

As our month of birth is always considered to be zero effective, auspicious events like marriages are avoided during the month of birth.

The Days (thithis) of Birth have Zero effect on the Zodiac sign on lifestyle. Accordingly...

Birth Day (Thithis)	Zero effective sign/Rasi
1. Prathama	Libra (Thulam) Capricorn (Makaram)
2. Dwitiya	Sagittarius (Dhanus) Pisces (Meenam)
3. Tritiya	Capricorn (Makaram) Leo (Simmam)
4. Chaturti	Aquarius (Kumbham) Taurus (Rishabam)
5. Panchami	Gemini (Mithunam) Virgo (Kanni)
6. Shashthi	Aries (Mesham) Leo (Simmam)
7. Sapthami	Sagittarius (Dhanus) Cancer (Karkataka)
8. Ashtami	Gemini (Mithunam) Virgo (Kanni)
9. Navami	Leo (Simmam) Scorpio (Viruchigam)
10. Dasami	Scorpio (Viruchigam) Leo (Simmam)
11. Ekadasi	Sagittarius (Dhanus) Pisces (Meenam)
12. Dvadasi	Libra (Thulam) Capricorn (Makaram)
13. Trayodashi	Taurus (Rishabam) Leo (Simmam)
14. Chaturdashi	Gemini (Mithunam) Virgo (Kanya) Sagittarius (Dhanus) Pisces (Meenam)
15.	Both New Moon Day (Amavasya) and Full Moon Day (Purnima) are not affected and have full effect.

According to my research, the zero effect thithis extend certain relationships and has severe impacts.

Pisces Dwitiya Ekadasi Chaturdashi	**Aries** Shashti	**Taurus** Chaturti Trayodashi	**Gemini** Panchami Ashtami Chaturdashi
Aquarius Chaturti	**Signs/Rasis in Which Each thithis attaining Zero Effect/Effectless Are Given here**		**Cancer** Saptami
Capricorn Prathama Tritiya Dwadashi			**Leo** Tritiya Shashti Navami Dashami Thrayodashi
Sagittarius Dwitiya Saptami Ekadasi Chaturdashi	**Scorpio** Navami Dashami	**Libra** Prathama Dwadashi	**Virgo** Panchami Ashtami Chaturdashi

Asterisms/stars to have zero effect. Accordingly for each native, his birth star is effectless or has zero effect.

GANDANTHA AND DAY-NIGHT-DAY CONVERGENCE

Gandantha and Day-Night-Day Convergence duration is considered to be inauspicious and emphasises malediction.

Asterisms/Star-based Gandantha:

The near-end degrees of Pisces and the very beginning degrees of Aries. (29° - 30° of star Revathi in Pisces and 0° - 2° of star Aswini in Aries).

The near-end degrees of Cancer and the very beginning degrees of Leo. (29° - 30° of star Aslesha (Ayilyam) in Cancer and 0° - 2° of star Makam in Leo)

The near-end degrees of Scorpio and the very beginning degrees of Sagittarius. (29° - 30° of Jyeshta (Kettai) in Scorpio and 0° - 2° of star Moolam in Sagittarius).

The endpoint of a star and the beginning point of another star is termed Gandantha degrees.

Day-Night-Day Convergence

The duration of the ending of daytime and beginning of Night and similarly ending of Night time and beginning of a day is termed as time Convergence.

Children born during these inauspicious times carry malediction along with them.

Sexual Unions during the mentally disturbed period result in the birth of children with malediction. Hence clear undisturbed peaceful environment during sexual union/intercourse is considered good and healthy.

STARS AND UNSTABLE LONGEVITY (SHORT LIFE/ MISFORTUNE)

Children born in Stars Pushya (Poosam), Chitra 2nd part, Purvashada 3rd part, Revathy 3rd part, Uthira Phalguni 1st Part (Uthiram) bring unstable longevity which may be in the form of short life or misfortune to its parents and relatives.

UNSTABLE LONGEVITY (SHORT LIFE/MISFORTUNE) BASED ON PLANETARY POSITIONS:

1. Position of Natal Moon close to Rahu/Ketu in Natal (Birth) Chart/Horoscope

2. Position of Natal Maha Dasa (Dasa) Lord in close position to Rahu/Ketu in Natal (Birth) Chart/Horoscope

3. Position of Natal Moon and Maha Dasa (Dasa) Lord near the lord of the 8th (Ashtamathipathi) or lord of the evil (Bhadagathipathi) 11th, 9th, or 7th according to the movable, Fixed or Dual (Upaya) ascendants.

4. Birth of children in Star-based Gandantha

5. Combust positions/placements of Lord of Ascendant/ Sign (Rasi)

6. Positioning of malefic like Rahu or Ketu, Mars, Saturn in trines to Jupiter or Moon in natal (birth) Chart/ horoscope.

All the above six planetary positions/placements indicate unstable longevity (Short Life/misfortune)

SHORT LIFE SPAN OF CHILDREN OR DEATH IN CHILDHOOD

Death threat in children during young age before 12 years

Sl. No	Age of the Child	Reason for Death threat
1	0 – 1 Year	Past Karma of the Child
2	1 – 4 Years	Karma of the mother
3	4 – 8 Years	Karma of the father
4	8 – 12 Years	Present Karma of the Child

Sl. No	Sign/Rasi	Severity in degrees	Star
1	Aries	28	Krittika
2	Taurus	09	Krittika
3	Gemini	22	Ardra (Thiruvadhirai)
4	Cancer	22	Ashlesha (Ayilyam)
5	Leo	05	Makam
6	Virgo	01	Uttara Phalguni (Uthiram)
7	Libra	04	Chitra (Chithirai)
8	Scorpio	23	Jyeshta (Kettai)
9	Sagittarius	18	Purva Ashada (Pooradam)
10	Capricorn	20	Shravana (Tiruvonam)
11	Aquarius	21	Shatabhisha (Sadayam)
12	Pisces	10	Purva Bhadrapada (Purattathi)

Placement/position of the Moon or ascendant lord in the above signs/Rasi and degrees cause death threat to the Children.

The Planetary positions in the above signs cause death threats or disability/ill health in children at a very early stage.

IS THE BIRTH-TIME, CORRECT?

This question will ordinarily pop up in many people including astrologers.

Old astrological treatises have mentioned 'KUNDA NIGNA METHOD', which matches the current trend.

What is 'KUNDA NIGNA METHOD'?

The establishment of a strong relationship between the natal ascendant and the natal Moon is termed a 'KUNDA NIGNA METHOD'.

Adana Lagna's (ascendant) computation is the best as it is a time calculation based on the time of conception.

Adana Lagna (ascendant) is the exact time it takes to ejaculate during vaginal penetration.

An evaluation by matching the natal Moon coupled with the Adana ascendant **TO the** natal ascendant coupled with the natal Moon is the Adana assessment method.

If the Adana time ascendant degrees match equally with the natal Moon the child will be born in 273 days.

If the natal Moon's position in degrees matches with the Adana time Moon's degrees and Adana period 7th bhavaga degrees the child will be born in 258 days.

If the natal Moon's position in degrees matches with Adana period 9th bhavaga degrees, then the child will be born in 287.14 days.

Ascendant indicated by Adana Moon	Pregnancy Period
Portion 1 Stage I of the Fetus	248 Days to 252 Days
Portion 1 Stage II of the Fetus	253 Days to 258 Days
Portion 2 Stage I of the Fetus	260 Days to 266 Days
Portion 2 Stage II of the Fetus	266 Days to 274 Days
Portion 2 Stage III of the Fetus	274 Days to 280 Days
Portion 3 Stage I of the Fetus	280 Days to 287 Days
Portion 3 Stage II of the Fetus	288 Days to 294 Days
Portion 3 Stage III of the Fetus	294 Days to 301 Days

When the position of the natal Moon in degrees equals the Adana Lagna (Ascendant) degrees the child will be born in 273 Days.

During Waxing Natal Moon, the seventh Bhavaga position in degrees of the natal Moon will be the Adana Lagna (ascendant) in degrees.

During Waning Natal Moon, the seventh Bhavaga position in degrees of the natal Moon will be the Adana Lagna (ascendant) in degrees.

When the Waxing natal Moon is positioned in more than the 7th Bhavaga degrees, the birth duration will be below 273 days.

When the Waxing natal Moon is positioned in less than the 7th Bhavaga degrees, the birth duration will be more than 273 days.

When the Warning natal Moon is positioned in less than the 7th Bhavaga degrees, the birth duration will be less than 273 days.

When the Waxing Moon is positioned in more than that of the 7th Bhavaga degrees, the birth duration will be less than 273 days.

When the Waxing Moon is positioned in less than that of the 7th Bhavaga degrees, the birth duration will be more than 273 days.

When the Waning Moon is positioned in more than that of the 7th Bhavaga degrees, the birth duration will be more than 273 days.

When the Waning Moon is positioned in less than that of the 7th Bhavaga degrees, the birth duration will be less than 273 days.

Likewise so, there are so many Adana experimental ways to judge the exact birth time wherein we have discussed only a few options here.

If the natal Moon is in the Waxing stage, the Adana Lagna (ascendant) is the same as that of the degrees in which the Moon is posited.

If the natal Moon is Waning, then the degree where the Moon is posited is the 7th Bhavaga position.

This resembles the Ruling Planet as per Krishnamoorthi Paddathi.

I have undertaken extensive and intense research regarding Adana's experimentation methods with the exclusive assistance of my research students. The Adana Lagna (ascendant) should be reconciled at all stages of the Day, Asterism (star), thithis, and ascendant by analysis.

Notes:

To get rid of the short span of life in children (Early death of a child) ...

For those with the (malediction) threat of a short span of life in children (Early death), every year fire rituals for longevity should be done on their birth star (asterism).

These rituals could be performed in Lord Shiva's temples using the best pandits.

The rituals give the best results when performed in the Local Ayyapan temple saving expenditures.

PLANETARY POSITIONS THAT FORBID BENEFITS OF FATHER'S PROPERTIES

If in a natal (birth) chart/horoscope of a child...

1. Placement of Venus in the stars of U.Phalguni (Uthiram), and Revathi

2. Placement of Jupiter in Visakam, Uthrashada (Uthiradam), and Uthra Bhadra (Uthirattathi)

3. Placement of Mercury or Mars in the stars Purvashada (Pooradam), and Purva Bhadra

Forbid enjoyment of the benefits of Father's properties.

Even one of the three conditions mentioned above will render the rule valid.

The above conditions may seem to be ordinary at a preliminary outlook but match in 27 natal (birth) charts of the 30 horoscopes analysed proving a 75% success level in practice.

It can be affirmed that planets posited in a few stars cause such problems.

STELLIUM OR PLANETARY WAR

To assess the strength of planets in a natal (birth) chart/ horoscope, the stellium is a very important factor among others. Mars, Mercury, Jupiter, Venus, and Saturn are the five important planets that will play a vital role in the stellium and determine the strength of the natal (birth) chart.

Planets posited in close degrees say within 3 degrees within themselves are considered to be involved in stellium or a war.

Victory or loss in the War is equally applicable here. Those Planets which are posited in high degrees are declared as winners and those posited in low degrees are the losers.

The Planets who were adjudged as winners (posited in high degrees) in the planetary war extend the best beneficial results and those who lost in the war (posited in low degrees) extend poor or malefic results.

If the planet which has lost in the war happens to be the lord of the 5th who is responsible for progeny, it bestows only malefic malediction such as childless status or differently abled/special children.

For Example,

Let us assume Mars is posited at 6° and Saturn at 4° (both placed within 3°) in Leo. Here Mars is placed in high degrees than Saturn declaring Mars as the winner and Saturn as the loser in the planetary war.

LORD OF THE FIFTH BHAVAGA

Rule 1:

If the lord of the 5th is posited in between two malefic planets, it will cause malediction or misery through children.

Rule 2:

If the lord of the 5th is posited close to the inimical planets of the 5th lord, then it will cause misery through children.

Rule 3:

If planets inimical to the lord of the 5th are posited in the 5th position from the lord of the 5th house, it will cause misery through children.

Example 1

		Ketu	
	Birth		
Mars	Example 1		Ascendant
5	Rahu		Saturn

Example 2

	Mars	Saturn	Ketu
	Birth		
	Example 2		
Rahu			Ascendant

Example 1 to establish Rule 1

In this Leo ascendant natal (birth) chart, Sagittarius Sign/ Rasi is placed between two malefic planets which is the 5th house from the ascendant and according to Rule 1, this proves a big malediction through children.

Example 2 to establish Rule 2

Our Rule 2 indicates that when the lord of the 5th is placed between two inimical planets, it causes severe malediction and misery in children. In the above natal (birth) chart 2, Saturn the lord of the 5th for Virgo ascendant is between two malefic Mars and Ketu which is like caught between an evil pair of scissors proving the existence of malediction through children.

In the above example natal (birth) chart, the 5th house lord Saturn is already an inimical and slow planet. Here Saturn has dual authority as the lord of the 5th and lord of the evil 6th bhavaga inheriting more power to delay progeny and with added malediction by its placement in between an evil pair of scissors, the very dangerous and inimical planets Mars ad Ketu.

Even if benefic Jupiter throws its aspect on the 5th house or Saturn, in such placement Saturn is sure to execute its malefic effect.

<table>
<tr><td colspan="2"></td><td></td><td></td></tr>
<tr><td rowspan="2"></td><td rowspan="2" colspan="2">Birth

Example 3</td><td></td></tr>
<tr><td>Mars

Sun</td><td></td></tr>
<tr><td></td><td></td><td></td><td>Ascendant

Saturn</td></tr>
</table>

Example chart 3 to establish Rule 3

In the above Virgo ascendant Chart, the 5th lord Saturn is posited in the ascendant itself and its two inimical planets Mars and the Sun are placed in Saturn's 5th house (trine). As per the rule of the existence of malediction which operates when inimical planets are posited in the 5th house (trines) to the lord of the 5th house, this chart proves to carry malediction in having children and misery through children. In addition to this, the placement of any two of the four inimical planets Saturn, Mars, Rahu, and Ketu in the 5th house to the 5th house lord stresses the existence of malediction through children.

A scrutiny of example chart 2 indicates that the 5th house lord Saturn is moving towards its all the more inimical Ketu rather than its placement in between evil pair of scissors giving more vital stress.

More importantly, it is the approach of Ketu towards Saturn, the 5th house lord which enhances malediction in having children. It is something like the thrashing of a person who was caught and held by two.

Hence the position of the 5th house and the lord of the 5th house in many stages before declaring good or bad results about progeny.

19

EXCHANGE OF HOUSES AND PROGENY

The exchange of houses is considered the transfer of two planets occupying each other's own houses or the stars owned by them.

Such exchange of houses may either be beneficial or extend unfortunate results.

Results from an exchange of houses...

1. Unexpected conception against the devoid of progeny.

2. Death of a child in an unexpectant situation. (Death of the child in an environment where the supposed person escapes death.)

3. Unexpected Conception after medical treatment against declared childless position in a couple. (Conception after treatment for uterus-related problems or through artificial methods like IVF and others).

As an example, take a look at the natal (birth) chart/ horoscope of a woman given below:

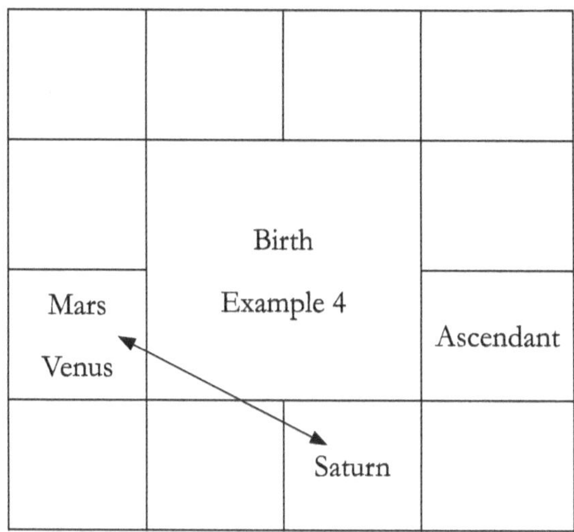

In the example chart of a lady, Venus and Saturn have exchanged their houses. She remained childless for up to two years and delivered a male baby after medical treatment for her uterus-related problems.

Another example chart is given below:

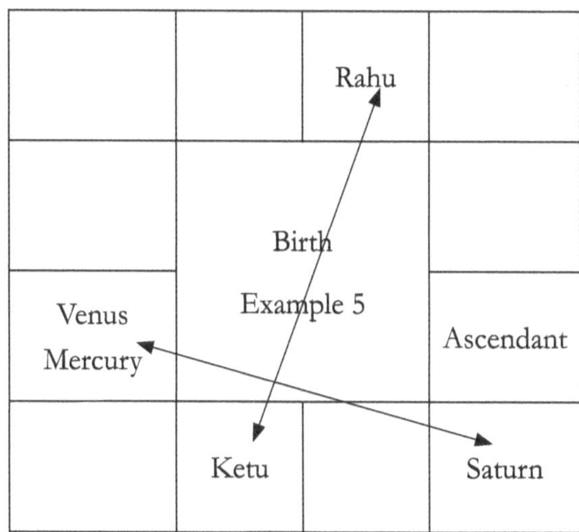

In the above natal (birth) chart/horoscope of a man, Saturn and Mercury have exchanged their houses. He remained childless for six years and took medical treatment for strengthening sperm to procreate a baby girl.

He undertook medical treatment only after realizing that he is sterile and unable to give birth to a child.

Notes:

A planet which has exchanged its house will cause deadly sequences while passing over inimical planets Rahu/Ketu. Passing/crossing over Rahu/Ketu mentions the presence of Rahu/Ketu next to the house which has exchanged its place with another planet. A close look at example 5 shows that Saturn who has exchanged its home with Mercury has to meet/pass over Ketu which is approaching it from Scorpio.

20

PLANETARY PARENTHESIS IN COUPLES

According to our research, the planetary parenthesis in the joint horoscopes/natal (birth) charts of the couples should be evaluated with care.

Planetary parenthesis in couples means...

1. Position of Rahu/Ketu in high degrees in the natal (birth) chart of the husband than the position of Jupiter in degrees in the wife's horoscope cause malediction in having children for the couples. Even the non-existence of defects in the individual charts of the husband and wife may transform into a malediction in having children when the planetary parenthesis of the couple is considered as a combined/joint horoscope.

2. Placement of Rahu/Ketu, Mars, or Saturn in the same sign/Rasi of the husband in which the Moon is positioned in the sign/Rasi of the wife endorses malediction in having children for the couples.

3. Affliction of the lord of the 5th in the couple's horoscope/ natal (birth) chart show causes of malediction in having children.

Example 1

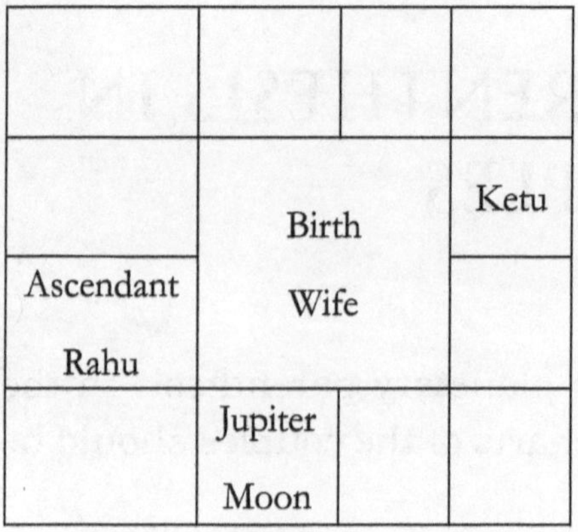

<table>
<tr><td></td><td colspan="2"></td><td rowspan="2">Ketu</td><td></td></tr>
<tr><td rowspan="2">Ketu</td><td colspan="2" rowspan="2">Birth

Wife</td><td></td></tr>
<tr><td rowspan="2">Birth

Husband</td><td rowspan="2">Ascendant</td></tr>
</table>

	Birth Wife	Ketu
Ascendant Rahu		
	Jupiter Moon	

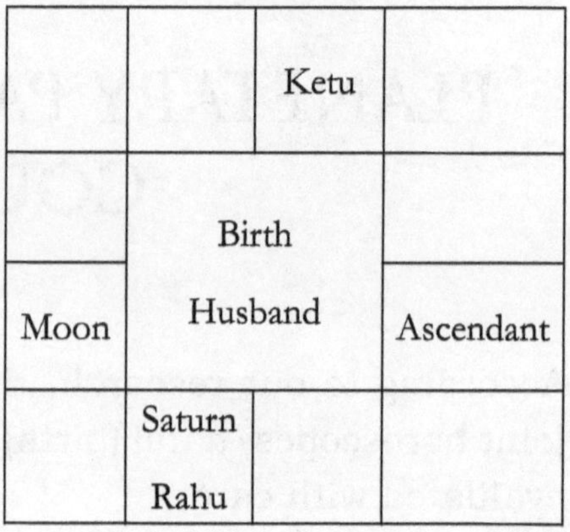

	Ketu	
Moon	Birth Husband	Ascendant
	Saturn Rahu	

In the above natal (birth) chart of the husband, Saturn and Rahu, the two inimical planets are posited in Scorpio where Jupiter is posited in the natal (birth) chart/horoscope of the wife which establishes strong malediction in having children. As Jupiter and the Moon are placed in the wife's horoscope/natal (birth) chart in Scorpio, it is very important to fix the marriage at a time when inimical planets in transit are not posited in Scorpio to avoid such a malediction.

Sl. No	Wife	Husband
1	Jupiter in Scorpio	Rahu in Scorpio
2	Moon in Scorpio	Saturn in Scorpio
3	Capricorn Ascendant	Leo Ascendant
4	Rahu in Capricorn	Moon in Capricorn

As the Capricorn Moon of the Husband is over the Rahu posited in the same Capricorn in the wife's natal (birth) chart, it indicates severe malediction in having children by the couple.

It is equally important that the lord of the 5th house who is responsible for progeny for both husband and wife should not be placed in the 6th and 8th houses between them. In the above example, both the husband and wife have such 6th and 8th house placement in the grip of inimical planets.

Ways to assess the planets when malediction in having children exist according to the Bhavaga method

1. Planets Saturn and Rahu/Ketu are in the same sign as the other where one has natal Jupiter indicating the existence of severe malediction through children. Hence the marriage should be fixed at a time when no inimical transit planets pass over the sign where natal Jupiter is posited.

2. Planets Saturn and Rahu/Ketu are in the same sign as the other where one has a natal Moon indicating the existence of severe malediction through children. Hence the marriage should be fixed at a time when no inimical transit planets pass over the sign where the natal Moon is posited.

3. If Saturn is posited in the 5th house of both husband and wife in their individual natal (birth) chart, it causes severe malediction in having children.

4. Both husband and wife should not have their natal (birth) chart placed at the Sashta-Ashta position which is 6th and 8th or 8th and 6th between them which does not show mental/intune compatibility between the couple.

5. If Saturn's aspect or associated with the lord of the 8th or lord of the evil 11th house, it will cause severe malediction in having children.

Example 2

In the below given natal chart of the husband, ruling Saturn conjoined with Ketu is posited in the Capricorn sign which has debilitated Jupiter in the same Capricorn sign of the natal chart of the wife.

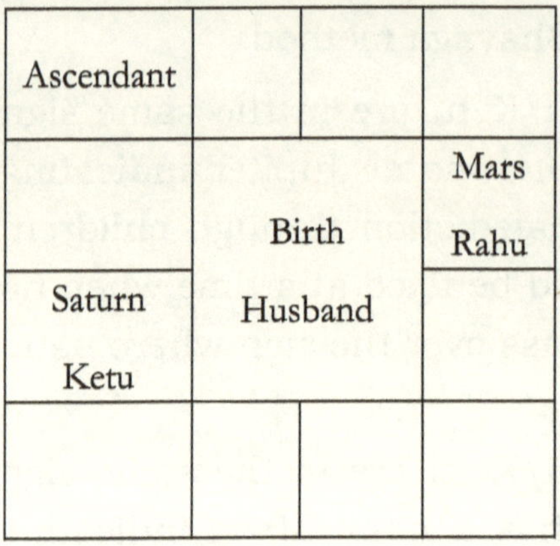

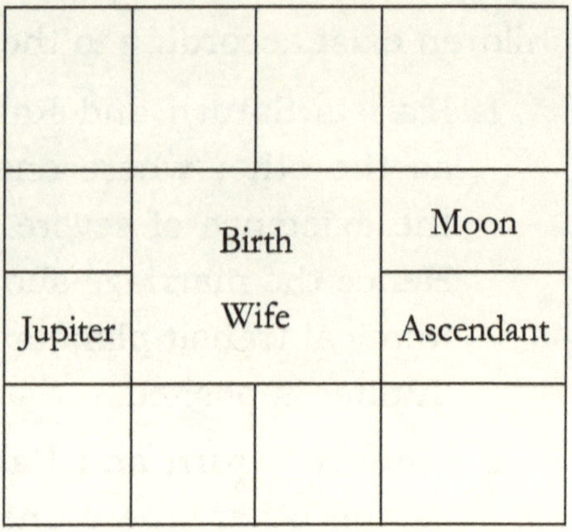

<table>
<tr><td>Ascendant</td><td></td><td></td><td></td></tr>
<tr><td rowspan="2"></td><td rowspan="2" colspan="2">Birth
Husband</td><td>Mars

Rahu</td></tr>
<tr><td></td></tr>
<tr><td>Saturn

Ketu</td><td></td></tr>
<tr><td></td><td></td><td></td><td></td></tr>
</table>

<table>
<tr><td></td><td></td><td></td><td>Moon</td></tr>
<tr><td>Jupiter</td><td colspan="2">Birth
Wife</td><td>Ascendant</td></tr>
<tr><td></td><td></td><td></td><td></td></tr>
</table>

In the husband's natal (birth) chart, debilitated Mars and Rahu are placed in Cancer which has a strong ruling Moon in the wife's natal (birth) chart. The ascendants of both husband and wife are posited in the 6th and 8th position in between them inducing strong malediction in having children for both husband and wife. Hence, the wife could not conceive for several years and had miscarriages 14 times.

Notes:

The person with the curse of the nodes Rahu and Ketu fed milk to the anthill and ants as a remedial measure. She conceived after that. She now leads a happy life with her children.

21

MRITHYU (DEADLIER PART) CALCULATION IN DEGREES

Mrithyu's part in degrees indicates severe deadlier/distress consequences in a person. This position is calculated in two ways.

1. Based on certain specific degrees of an asterism/star in a Sign/Rasi which will not alter and be fixed from the time of Birth.

2. Based on the Sun's position in degrees and the day of reckoning.

Sl. No	Sign/Rasi	Mrithyu degrees	Part of the Star
1	Aries	8	Aswini 3
2	Taurus	9	Kritika 4
3	Gemini	11	Arudra (Thiruvadhirai)
4	Cancer	11	Pushya (Poosam)
5	Leo	25	Purva Phalguna (Pooram)
6	Virgo	4, 11	Uthra Phalguna (Uthiram) Hastham 3, 4
7	Libra	4	Chithra 4
8	Scorpio	25	Jyeshta 3 (Kettai 3)
9	Sagittarius	18	Purvashada 2 (Pooradam 2)
10	Capricorn	2	Uthrashada 2 (Uthiradam 2)
11	Aquarius	21	Purva Bhadra 1 (Poorattathi 1)
12	Pisces	11	Uthra Bhadra 3 (Uthirattathi 3)

If a planet is posited in Mrithyu point degrees during birth in the natal chart, it will cause havoc during its Maha Dasa (Dasa), or Anthar Dasa (Bukthi).

If Moon is placed in the Mrithyu point degrees in the natal (birth) chart, it shows a threat to life. If the 5th house lord is placed in the mrithyu point degrees in the natal (birth) chart of both husband and wife, they beget physically or mentally challenged (like autism) children.

To arrive at the Mrithyu point:

1. The position of the Sun in degrees.

2. Whether the Mrithyu point is for the Day or Night time.

3. This is dependent on the birth time and Day of the week.

Sl. No	Day	Mrithyu degrees are to be added for Day time	Mrithyu degrees are to be added for Night time
1	Sunday	60	312
2	Monday	36	288
3	Tuesday	12	264
4	Wednesday	156	240
5	Thursday	132	216
6	Friday	108	192
7	Saturday	84	336

The above table **indicates the degrees of the Day time and Night time of the Days with which the Sun's position in degrees is to be added to get the Mrithyu point in degrees.**

The easy way to remember the Mrithyu point in degrees for Daytime.

Given below is an easy way to remember the Daytime Mrithyu point in degrees. A day consists of 24 hours.

To start with, the Mrithyu point in degrees for TUESDAY is 12 and by adding 24 to this the resultant 36 degrees is the Mrithyu point in degrees for MONDAY.

The Mrithyu point in degrees for MONDAY is 36 and by adding 24 to this the resultant 60 degrees is the Mrithyu point in degrees for SUNDAY.

The Mrithyu point in degrees for SUNDAY is 60 and by adding 24 to this the resultant 84 degrees is the Mrithyu point in degrees for SATURDAY

The Mrithyu point in degrees for SATURDAY is 84; by adding 24 to this, the resultant 108 degrees is the Mrithyu point in degrees for FRIDAY.

The Mrithyu point in degrees for FRIDAY is 108; by adding 24 to this, the resultant 132 degrees is the Mrithyu point in degrees for THURSDAY.

The Mrithyu point in degrees for THURSDAY is 132 and by adding 24 to this the resultant 156 degrees is the Mrithyu point in degrees for WEDNESDAY.

The Day begins on Tuesday with Mrithyu pointing in 12 degrees and going in descending order of the day with an increase of 24 degrees each day.

The easy way to remember the Mrithyu point in degrees for Night time.

Given below is an easy way to remember Night time Mrithyu points in degrees. A day consists of 24 hours.

To start with, the Mrithyu point in degrees for FRIDAY is 192 and by adding 24 to this the resultant 216 degrees is the Mrithyu point in degrees for THURSDAY.

The Mrithyu point in degrees for THURSDAY is 216 and by adding 24 to this the resultant 240 degrees is the Mrithyu point in degrees for WEDNESDAY.

The Mrithyu point in degrees for WEDNESDAY is 240 and by adding 24 to this the resultant 264 degrees is the Mrithyu point in degrees for TUESDAY.

The Mrithyu point in degrees for TUESDAY is 264; by adding 24 to this, the resultant 288 degrees is the Mrithyu point in degrees for MONDAY.

The Mrithyu point in degrees for MONDAY is 288; by adding 24 to this, the resultant 312 degrees is the Mrithyu point in degrees for SUNDAY.

The Mrithyu point in degrees for SUNDAY is 312 and by adding 24 to this the resultant 336 degrees is the Mrithyu point in degrees for SATURDAY.

The Day begins on FRIDAY with Mrithyu pointing at 192 degrees and going in descending order of the day with an increase of 24 degrees each day.

Mrithyu points to distress or sorrow one undergoes/ will undergo.

Example:

Let us now calculate the Mrithyu point in degrees for Daytime on a Thursday.

The Sun's position = 145°

The daytime Mrithyu point for Thursday = 132°

The resultant Mrithyu point = 145° + 132° = 277°

This 277° indicates the asterism/star Uthrashada (Uthiradam) in Capricorn sign/Rasi.

Calculation of Mrithyu point n degrees during the Night time on a Thursday

The Sun's position = 145°

The Night time Mrithyu point for Thursday = 216°

The resultant Mrithyu point = 145° + 216° = 361° which is more than 360°.

Deducting 360° net effect is 361° - 360° = 1° which indicates the star Aswini in Aries.

Important Note:

It is very important to note the calculation of Mrithyu point for Day time or Night time and when it is added to the Sun's position in degrees, a deduction of 360° should be done when it exceeds 360°. This is necessary.

The results of Mrithyu point in degrees

If the starting point of the indicator of progeny, 5th Bhavaga falls on the Mrithyu point in degrees, the child so born extends unbearable extreme sorrow to the parents.

Example

I analysed a horoscope in the year presented to me by my mentor and Guide Shri. Nataraj of Oddanchatiram in the year 2008.

The planet posited in the Mrithyu point degrees in the Purva Phalguna asterism (Pooram star) in Leo Sign/Rasi was running its Maha Dasa (Dasa).

I cautioned him about many Mrithyu maledictions during that period which came true and he suffered a lot to get rid of the problems caused.

If the Mrithyu malediction exists in the natal (birth) chart of the child, it affects both the child and its parents.

Instead, if it exists in the natal (birth) chart of the parents, it affects only the parents forcing them to face severe problems.

22

CALCULATION OF MANTI (PLANETOID OR UPAGRAHA)

How do reckon Manti as? Manti is a Upagraha or Planetoid who causes irreparable losses or unbearable malediction. He is distinguished as the son of Saturn who obstructs and prevents progeny. Many couples remain childless due to the existence of malediction by Manti. In the olden days, the native (birth) charts were cast without any mention of Manti and declared the results without attaching much importance to Manti. But now Manti gets due importance and finds a place in the natal (birth) chart which is a welcome feature.

To Know the Manti point in degrees

Sl. No	Day	Manti degrees are to be added for Day time	Manti degrees are to be added for Night time
1	Sunday	156	240
2	Monday	132	216
3	Tuesday	108	192
4	Wednesday	84	336
5	Thursday	60	312
6	Friday	36	288
7	Saturday	12	264

1. The Sun's position in degrees should be known

2. It should be identified whether Manti's position should be known for the Day time or Night time.

3. The Manti's position in degrees should be added with the Sun's position in degrees.

The easy way to remember the Manti point in degrees for Daytime.

Given below is an easy way to remember the Daytime Manti point in degrees. A day consists of 24 hours.

To start with, the MANTI point in degrees for SATURDAY is 12 and by adding 24 to this the resultant 36 degrees is the MANTI point in degrees for FRIDAY.

The MANTI point in degrees for FRIDAY is 36; by adding 24 to this, the resultant 60 degrees is the MANTI point in degrees for THURSDAY.

The MANTI point in degrees for THURSDAY is 60; by adding 24 to this, the resultant 84 degrees is the MANTI point in degrees for WEDNESDAY.

The MANTI point in degrees for WEDNESDAY is 84; by adding 24 to this, the resultant 108 degrees is the MANTI point in degrees for TUESDAY.

The MANTI point in degrees for TUESDAY is 108; by adding 24 to this, the resultant 132 degrees is the MANTI point in degrees for MONDAY.

The MANTI point in degrees for MONDAY is 132; by adding 24 to this, the resultant 156 degrees is the MANTI point in degrees for SUNDAY.

The Day begins on Saturday with Manti pointing in 12 degrees and going in descending order of the day with an increase of 24 degrees each day.

The easy way to remember the Manti point in degrees for Night time.

Given below is an easy way to remember Night time Manti points in degrees. A day consists of 24 hours.

To start with, the MANTI point in degrees for FRIDAY is 192 and by adding 24 to this the resultant 216 degrees is the MANTI point in degrees for THURSDAY.

The MANTI point in degrees for THURSDAY is 216; by adding 24 to this, the resultant 240 degrees is the MANTI point in degrees for WEDNESDAY.

The MANTI point in degrees for WEDNESDAY is 240 and by adding 24 to this the resultant 264 degrees is the MANTI point in degrees for TUESDAY.

The MANTI point in degrees for TUESDAY is 264; by adding 24 to this, the resultant 288 degrees is the MANTI point in degrees for MONDAY.

The MANTI point in degrees for MONDAY is 288; by adding 24 to this, the resultant 312 degrees is the MANTI point in degrees for SUNDAY.

The MANTI point in degrees for SUNDAY is 312 and by adding 24 to this the resultant 336 degrees is the MANTI point in degrees for SATURDAY.

The Day begins on FRIDAY with Mrithyu pointing at 192 degrees and going in descending order of the day with an increase of 24 degrees each day.

Manti points at the deadly sequences, distress, sorrow, and curses inherited from the forefathers and ancestors.

Important Note:

While computing Manti, it has to be taken note of whether it is for Day time or Night time. When the Sun's position in degrees is added, 360° should be deducted when the combined result is more than 360°.

Let us now calculate the Manti point in degrees for Daytime on a Thursday.

The Sun's position = 145°

The daytime Manti point for Thursday = 132°

The resultant Manti point = 145° + 132° = 277°

This 277° indicates the asterism/star Uthrashada (Uthiradam) in Capricorn sign/Rasi.

When the 5th Bhavaga lord becomes the Sun and conjoins Manti

It indicates malediction through paternal inheritance.

It also refers to the infringement or interference in administration leading to maladministration and resultant effects.

When the 5th Bhavaga lord becomes the Moon and conjoins Manti

It indicates malediction through maternal inheritance.

It indicates the curse of women who were ill-treated, insulted, loses, dishonoured, and disgraced and who were very affectionate like a mother.

When the 5th Bhavaga lord becomes Mars and conjoins Manti

It indicates malediction through the siblings (Brothers and Sisters).

It indicates the curse of people who were ill-treated, insulted, loses, dishonour, and disgraced and who were very affectionate like a brother/sister.

It also denotes malediction acquired by cheating in the name of providing security.

When the 5th Bhavaga lord is Mercury and conjoins Manti

It denotes the curse/malediction through maternal/ paternal uncles.

When the 5th Bhavaga lord is Jupiter and conjoins Manti

Here, malediction/curse is very severe as both the Karaka lord and the 5th Bhavaga lord are Jupiter himself.

It indicates the curse of a person who was ill-treated, insulted, loses, dishonoured, and disgraced and who was very affectionate like a child/father/preceptor.

When the 5th Bhavaga lord is Saturn and conjoins Manti

It indicates malediction through subordinates/servants/labourers.

This malediction is the result of betrayal in the work entrusted to one's self.

When the 5th Bhavaga lord is Rahu/Ketu and conjoins Manti

This denotes malediction through excessive lust and greed.

This malediction is the result of cheating, thievery, stealing, and lying, thus causing mental stress and pain to others.

23

JUPITER'S MOVEMENT CAUSES A MALEDICTION IN PROGENY AS KARAKA FOR CHILD

Jupiter as the Karaka lord for progeny while moving towards Rahu or Ketu causes severe distress/sorrow through children or delays conception.

Even if Rahu or Ketu is away many Signs/Rasis from Jupiter, it stresses the existence of malediction/curse through children if Jupiter touches Rahu/Ketu at first. This rule strongly emphasises the need for no presence of any other planets in between Jupiter and Rahu/Ketu.

The movement of the 5th Bhavaga lord towards the inimical Rahu/Ketu too indicates the curse/malediction through children and delay in progeny.

Even if empty houses are carrying no planets in between Rahu/Ketu and the 5th Bhavaga Lord, malediction/curse does exist if the 5th Bhavaga move and touches Rahu/Ketu first. Malediction/curse is effective only when no planets in between the lord of the 5th Bhavaga and Rahu/Ketu.

Example: 1

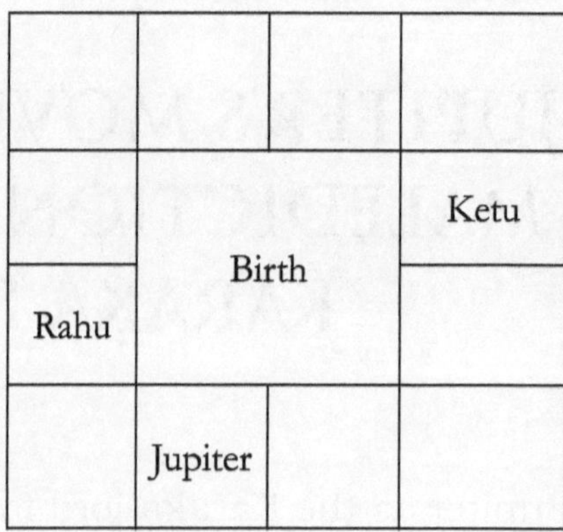

In the first chart, Jupiter is in Aquarius and Rahu in Pisces, in between them no other planets are establishing the existence of malediction/curse in having children.

In the next chart, Jupiter is in Scorpio and Rahu in Capricorn with empty Sagittarius in between them indicating the existence of malediction/curse in having children.

Example: 2

In the above natal chart of the husband, Jupiter is in Libra and Rahu in Aquarius leaving the in-between squares blank with no planets. As per our rules, this is also a malediction/ curse-preventing progeny.

In the natal (birth) chart of the wife, Jupiter and Rahu are aligned together with no planets in between establishing severe malediction/curse in having children. The couple remained childless for 12 years.

Those with malediction/curse through children lament that they are in their native/ancestral town but their children are in faraway places/foreign land. They feel whether they can unite back with their children and put forth the question to me during consultation.

Some women complained to me that their children have not addressed them as mothers for 13 years and have grown up in their grandparent's house.

The pain felt by such parents having begotten such children is the result of the position of Jupiter and Rahu/ Ketu.

24

WHEN WILL THE CURSE/ MALEDICTION TAKE EFFECT?

The differential signs in between Jupiter and Rahu determine the time of effect.

This is computed from the time of the Marriage of the native.

For example

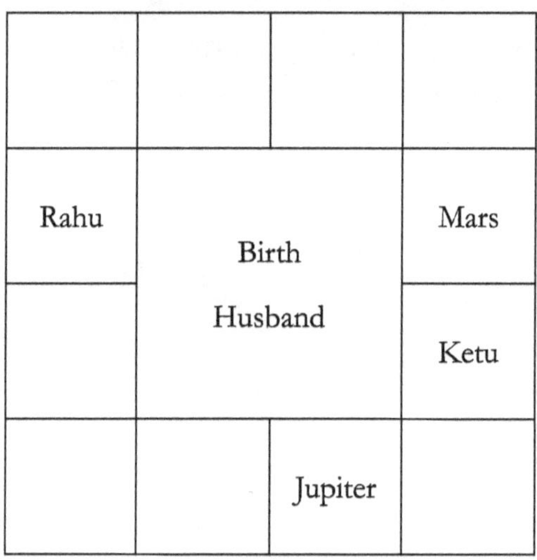

In the natal (birth) chart, Jupiter is posited in Libra and Rahu in Aquarius 5th house from Jupiter, showing a gap of 4 houses.

As Jupiter takes 12 years to complete a cycle, for four Signs/Rasis 4 x 12 = 48 years the native will be affected by the curse/malediction through children between 48 – 60 years of his age.

As per this rule...

When Jupiter and Rahu are in the same Sign/Rasi in the natal (birth) chart

The native will be affected by malediction/curse in having or through children between 0 – 12 years. One of his children may have some disability which will be disturbing the native mentally throughout his life.

When there are two signs/Rasis in between Jupiter and Rahu

The native will be affected between 12 and 24 years of age by the curse/malediction in begetting children/through children. The native will also face hurdles and hindrances in sourcing income for his children.

The native will face huge debt/financial issues and hurdles during the conduct of the marriage of the children.

When there are three Signs/Rasis in between Jupiter and Rahu

This native will undergo sufferings through malediction by not having children or through children from 24 years to 36 years.

When there are four Signs/Rasis in between Jupiter and Rahu

This native will suffer from 36 to 48 years of age due to malediction.

When there are five Signs/Rasis in between Jupiter and Rahu

Between 48 to 60 years of his age, the native will suffer the curse/malediction through children.

When there are Six Signs/Rasis in between Jupiter and Rahu

This native will face distress and sorrow from 48 years to 60 years of his age.

Somebody other than the native will be fond and secure the children of the native and when it goes beyond the limit there will be altercations or the child will be adopted.

When there are Seven Signs/Rasis in between Jupiter and Rahu

This Child will give sufferings/malediction to its parents from 0 to 12 years of its age.

When there are Eight Signs/Rasis in between Jupiter and Rahu

The native will suffer curse/malediction between 12 to 24 years of his age.

When there are Nine Signs/Rasis in between Jupiter and Rahu

The native will face distress/sorrow between 36 to 48 years of his age through children due to malediction.

When there are Ten Signs/Rasis in between Jupiter and Rahu

The native will suffer through curse/malediction in having children/through children through 36 to 48 years of his age.

When there are Eleven Signs/Rasis in between Jupiter and Rahu

The native will face distress/sorrow between 36 to 48 years of his age through children due to malediction.

When there are Twelve Signs/Rasis in between Jupiter and Rahu

The native will face distress/sorrow through malediction in having children/through children.

This bad period can be surpassed if the native remains unperturbed, generous without greed and seek spiritual realisation.

25

THE MOON AND MALEDICTION THROUGH CHILDREN

The immediate movement of the Karaka lord for progeny or the Moon's towards Rahu/Ketu causes intensive malediction through children or delayed progeny.

Even if there are several empty houses between the Moon and Rahu/Ketu, if the Moon touches Rahu/Ketu it causes severe blemish. The rule reiterates the absence of planets in between the Moon and Rahu/Ketu for the rule to take effect.

Example: 1

Rahu			
Moon	Birth		
	Husband		
		Jupiter	Ketu

		Rahu	
	Birth		
	Wife		
Moon	Ketu		

In the above natal (birth) chart of the husband, the Moon is in Aquarius and Rahu is in Pisces.

Here, the Moon moves on to touch Rahu at first which indicates the existence of malediction through children.

In the wife's horoscope, the Moon is posited in Sagittarius and Rahu is in Taurus and in between them no other planets are prompting the Moon to touch Rahu at first establishing the prevalence of the blemish in begetting children. When both the husband and wife have the existence of identical maledictions, the affliction is so severe.

When the above ideas were discussed in our Rasipuram and Chennai classes, a humpty number of natal (birth) charts/horoscopes were analysed and found to be true in 98% of cases.

This is the success of our Research.

Ketu			
	Birth	Mars	
Moon	Husband		
		Rahu	

		Rahu	
Moon	Birth		
	Wife		
	Ketu		

When the Moon touches Ketu first instead of Rahu, the natives suffer distress and sorrow through children.

In the above example of the wife's natal (birth) chart, the Moon posited in Aquarius moves initially towards Rahu at Taurus and touches it first whereas, in the husband's natal (birth) chart, the Moon in Capricorn passes Aquarius to touch Rahu at Pisces as there are no planets between them.

The above position indicates the distress and sorrow both the husband and wife have to suffer the malediction through children as they remain childless for more than 13 years, they surpassed the entire 13 years period in medical treatment but have yet to beget children.

26

ZERO/CYPHER(VACUUM) (SOONYAM) THITHI

During the computation of the natal (birth) chart, a phrase called Zero/cypher(vacuum) (Soonyam) thithi finds a place which in a way is connected to the malediction through children.

When a child is born in Shasti thithi, the Signs afflicted are Aries and Leo.

Example: 1

	Birth		Jupiter (15.08°) Sun Rahu
Ketu			Mercury
	Ascendant		Moon (29.54°)

In the above natal (birth) chart, Mercury is in Leo which is considered as zero/cypher(vacuum) thithi giving ill effects to the native and he is currently running the (Mercury) Dasa.

In Cancer, Sun is posited at 20.55° and Jupiter at 15.08°

The Moon by occupying the highest degree of 29.54° in Virgo becomes the Atma Karaka.

The placement of Jupiter, the Sun, and Rahu in Cancer establishes the prevalence of severe malediction/blemish through children.

The Moon on its way touches the ascendant first and then Ketu.

Jupiter on its passage touches the Sun first and then Rahu. The native had four children. Let us now see how the native suffered malediction through his children.

The native had not communicated with his children for the past 17 years.

In his case, the malediction acted not as a blemish but gave distress and sorrow through children as he is born on Shasti thithi which denotes Aries and Leo as zero/cypher(vacuum) effective signs.

He is currently running Mercury Maha Dasa (Dasa) and this Dasa lord Mercury is posited in the zero/cypher(vacuum) effective sign/rasi compelling the native to undergo the stress of distress through children the entire 17 years Mercury Maha Dasa (Dasa) period.

If good fortunes or maledictions/distress/sorrow to take place on a native's natal (birth) chart/horoscope any one or two of the three factors – transit, Maha Dasa (Dasa), Anthar Dasa (Bukthi) should be in operation.

Neither good fortunes nor maledictions/distress/ blemishes will not show up when the distinctive transit, Maha Dasa (Dasa), or Anthar Dasa (Bukthi) are not in operation. Hence careful consideration is necessary before declaring the results.

Example: 2

Jupiter	Ketu	Moon	
Sun Mercury	Birth		Mars
Ascendant		Rahu	

In the above Sagittarius ascendant natal (birth) chart, the ascendant lord and 4th lord Jupiter is afflicted by zero/cypher(vacuum) thithi effect and is currently running his Maha Dasa (Jupiter Dasa).

The Sun is posited at 20.55°, the Moon at 19.00°, and Jupiter at 15.09°. In this natal (birth) chart, Jupiter is moving towards Ketu and touches it causing severe blemish in having/through children. Both Jupiter and Ketu are only 30° apart. The child is born and died in two hours.

Example: 3

Ketu Saturn			
	Birth		Ascendant
Jupiter			
		Moon	Rahu

Here Mercury is currently running the Maha Dasa (Dasa). For the Cancer ascendant, Capricorn and Libra are the zero/cypher(vacuum) defective thithi Signs/Rasis.

Debilitated Jupiter in Capricorn is in high degrees in the zero/cypher(vacuum) defective sign Capricorn for Cancer ascendant. Jupiter and Saturn have exchanged their houses. Jupiter who is also the 9th lord for Cancer ascendant has exchanged his house reflecting the zero/cypher(vacuum) defective thithi Sign.

As the ascendant lord Moon and 9th lord Jupiter are placed in zero/cypher(vacuum) defective thithi, the native has aggrieved thoughts and a relationship with his father. He had not spoken to his father for 21 years.

The Jupiter posited in zero/cypher(vacuum) afflicted thithi Capricorn in trines to Rahu joins Ketu after the exchange of houses with Saturn in Pisces which strengthens the affliction.

When a greater number of planets occupy the zero/ cypher(vacuum) afflicted thithi Signs/Rasis

In a child's natal (birth) chart, nearly six planets were connected with the zero/cypher(vacuum) afflicted thithi Signs/Rasis or Planets connected to zero/cypher(vacuum) afflicted thithi Signs.

The child's mother got married four times and made the child call her husband 'father' after successive marriages.

As the child kept changing calling to 'Father' somebody, it got wild listening to the word 'Father'. This is one of the reasons that cause the zero/cypher(vacuum) thithi affliction and a close follow-up of such aberrated behaviours in children will be a back effect of zero/cypher(vacuum) thithi affliction.

27

EXAMPLE FOR ZERO/CYPHER (VACUUM) AFFLICTED (SOONYAM) THITHI

The position of the 2nd and 5th house lords in zero/cypher(vacuum) afflicted thithis' cause inflict severe blemish/malediction in having/through children. On scrutiny amongst the natal (birth) charts in couples, the presence of lords of the 2nd and the 5th houses in zero/cypher(vacuum) afflicted thithis' delayed progeny/having descendants.

In the below given natal (birth) chart, the birth is on Thritiya whose zero/cypher(vacuum) affliction SignRasi related to it is Leo.

	Ascendant Rahu				Rahu		
Moon Jupiter	Female Sign/Rasi		Sun Mercury Venus	Jupiter Moon	Amsa		Mercury Sun Venus
Mars	Saturn	Ketu		Mars	Saturn	Ketu	

The lord of the 2nd house to Aries ascendant Venus is in Zero/cypher(vacuum) afflicted thithi (Soonya) Sign Leo.

The presence of the Sun and Saturn in watery signs Cancer and Scorpio delay progeny and their position in the same star/asterism of Saturn adds more pain by confirming the delayed progeny.

Given below is the natal chart of the lady's husband.

<table>
<tr><td>Jupiter</td><td></td><td></td><td>Ketu
Moon</td></tr>
<tr><td>Sun

Mars
Mercury</td><td colspan="2">Male</td><td>Ascendant</td></tr>
<tr><td>Rahu</td><td></td><td></td><td>Saturn</td></tr>
</table>

The Birth Day falls Ekadasi thithi for which the zero/cypher(vacuum) affliction thithi signs are Sagittarius and Pisces.

For Leo ascendant here, Sagittarius and Pisces are zero/cypher(vacuum) afflicted thithi signs and the 5th lord Jupiter is in 8th house Pisces and receipt of the aspect of Saturn a slow planet.

28

SATURN AND CHILDREN

1. Saturn's presence in the ascendant of the child gives distress and sorrow to its parents.

2. Saturn in the 2nd house gives distress and sorrow in its Middle Ages to the parents.

3. If Saturn contacts Jupiter + Mars combination or Jupiter conjoins Mars first in its initial movement, it gives distress/sorrow to children.

4. A Planet which is posited in a zero/cypher(vacuum) afflicted thithi sign extends severe blemish/distress through children during its Maha Dasa (Dasa). Anthar Dasa (Bukthi).

5. In the natal (birth) charts of couples if Saturn and the Sun are combined or aspect each other (For both husband and wife), it also exhibits severe blemish/malediction through children. This is the result of a deficiency in sperm counts or uterus-related problems in women.

Saturn dominated Children (In the natal (birth) charts).

Though they are affectionate towards their parents in their younger days, they fail to show or retain hatred towards their parents when they are grown up.

They cause a big division in the family before they turn 25 years of age.

They behave with their parents as mentally retarded.

Sun + Saturn combination in the horoscope/natal (birth) chart of women:

Such of those girl babies with Sun + Saturn combination in their natal (birth) charts are the darling of their father.

Example 1

<table>
<tr><td></td><td colspan="2">Ascendant</td><td></td><td></td><td></td><td></td><td>Sun

Saturn</td></tr>
<tr><td></td><td colspan="2" rowspan="2">Birth

Example 1</td><td></td><td></td><td colspan="2" rowspan="2">Birth

Example 2</td><td></td></tr>
<tr><td></td><td></td><td></td><td></td></tr>
<tr><td></td><td>Saturn

Sun</td><td></td><td></td><td></td><td></td><td></td><td></td></tr>
</table>

In the example chart 1 of a female, Saturn and the Sun are posited in the 7th house to Taurus ascendant. During the transit of Saturn to Gemini, the 2nd house to Taurus ascendant, she married against her father's will.

As the natal (birth) chart of the female had Saturn + Sun combination, her father was very affectionate to her and he could not resist his daughter's action but kept gazing at the marriage. He felt very much for his daughter's action but kept mum and desisted against expressing his ideas. But his daughter questioned him why he has not resisted her actions when she went against him.

Example 2

The example 2 chart is also that of a woman who is now 45 years old. Here too, Saturn conjoined the Sun in Gemini establishing the affectionate position of both father and daughter. Her father fulfilled all her wishes from her childhood as his dear darling. She was behaving just like a child.

Now she is forcing her father to get a divorce from her second husband whom she did not like childishly and is very stubborn in getting divorced.

Her father has not consulted any astrologer for his purpose, but now he is lamenting his over-affection towards his daughter which has put him now under pressure feeling for his son-in-law's precarious condition.

Example 3

<table>
<tr><td></td><td></td><td></td><td>Sun

Saturn

Moon</td></tr>
<tr><td></td><td rowspan="2" colspan="2">Birth

Example 3</td><td></td></tr>
<tr><td>Ascendant</td><td></td></tr>
<tr><td></td><td></td><td></td><td></td></tr>
</table>

The above-given natal (birth) chart is that of a girl (in 2018) who was just 16 years old and has the Moon, the Sun and Saturn in Gemini of Capricorn ascendant. She was very affectionate towards her father who regarded her as his darling. She used to eat snacks and junk foods entertained by her father in full.

This girl was affected by skin diseases and Doctors advised her to avoid junk and bakery items. Due to the conditions put forth by the Doctors, she stopped talking to her father which affected her father badly who is unable to concentrate on his work.

To keep the good terms with his daughter, he allowed her to continue eating bakery foods increasing her skin disease level which was beyond the point of revival leading to mental stress and strain on all the members of the family. The whole family including the father, mother, elder sister, and daughter have the combination of the Sun and Saturn conjunction in their natal (birth) chart.

In Male horoscopes/natal charts, the conjunction/ combination of the Sun and Saturn produces problems according to age.

In female natal (birth) charts/horoscopes the same Saturn and the Sun combination showers love and affection to their father depending on their age.

SUCCESSIVE BIRTHS OF ONLY FEMALE CHILDREN

When the Maha Dasa (Dasa) lord is currently running the Dasa when posited in an asterism/star owned by a female planet, or under the dominance of a female Planets, they beget only female children in succession.

		Ascendant					Ascendant
	Birth					Birth	
	Husband	Mars (P. Phalguna)				Wife	
							Sun (Hastham)

While the Mars Maha Dasa (Dasa) lord conducted his Dasa when in P. Phalguna asterism/star belonging to Venus for the Husband and the wife was running the Sun Maha Dasa (Dasa) which is posited in Hastha star in Virgo.

During the above Maha Dasa Period, the star lords are female Planets who blessed the couples with three female babies in succession.

30

POSITION OF MARS AND MONTHLY PERIOD PROBLEMS IN WOMEN

The Moon represents liquid materials and blood circulation.

The 3rd, 6th, 10th, and 11th houses from the ascendant are considered Upajayasthanas (Places of Victory) and their adjacent houses as the opposite (Negative or losses).

The women/females experience their monthly periods (menstruation) during the aspect of Mars over the transit of the Moon in apa jayasthanas (ill/negative) or the houses adjacent to upa jayasthanas.

After five days of menstruation, when husband and wife engage in sexual acts in good environmental temperament during the days when the natal (birth) chart Jupiter aspect the upa jayasthanas 3rd, 6th, 10th, or the 11th house, they beget good children through conception.

Any affliction to this 3rd, 6th, 10th, or 11th houses by the association/conjunction/aspect of inimical planets like Rahu/Ketu, Mars, or Saturn the conception or begetting children is delayed and malediction/blemish in having children and distress/sorrow through children takes place.

Example:

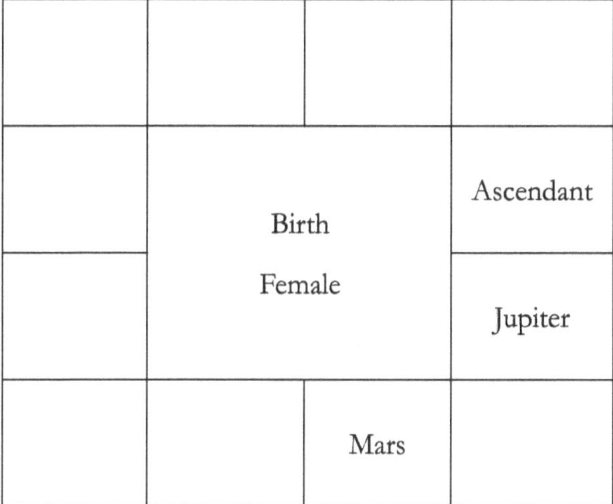

In the above natal (birth) chart of a woman, Mars is posited at Libra in the 4th house to cancer ascendant.

For Cancer ascendant, Virgo, Sagittarius, Aries, and Taurus are the Upajayasthanas 3rd, 6th, 10th, and 11th houses are the rest are apajayasthanas or the negative.

When the transit Moon passes over Capricorn receiving the 4th aspect of Mars, the woman will experience menstruation.

The sexual Union/intercourse of the couples during the transit days of Moon or Aries receiving the aspect of natal (birth) Jupiter will lead to conception in begetting a good child.

Planets that cause delay/irregular periods/disorders

- The Moon + Rahu conjunction/combination
- Mars + Rahu conjunction/combination
- Moon + Ketu conjunction/combination
- Mars + Ketu conjunction/combination
- Jupiter + Moon conjunction/combination

If the above combination is present in Scorpio or the 8th house from the ascendant or if Rahu/Ketu is present in the 7th house from the ascendant, then it will cause menstruation-related problems and disorders in females.

DISABILITY IN CHILDREN

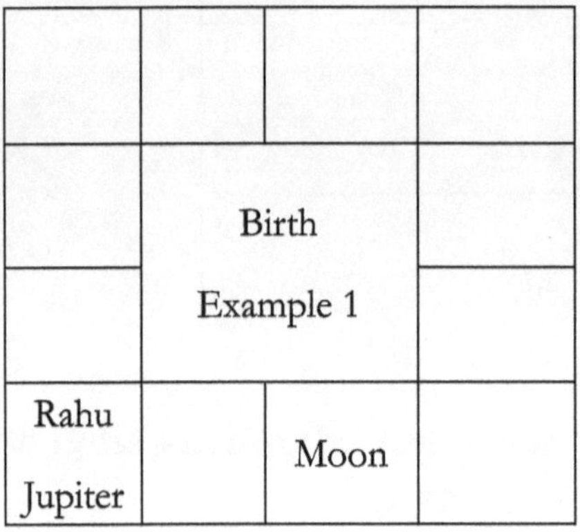

<table>
<tr><td></td><td></td><td></td><td></td></tr>
<tr><td></td><td colspan="2" rowspan="2">Birth

Example 1</td><td></td></tr>
<tr><td></td><td></td></tr>
<tr><td>Rahu

Jupiter</td><td>Moon</td><td></td><td></td></tr>
</table>

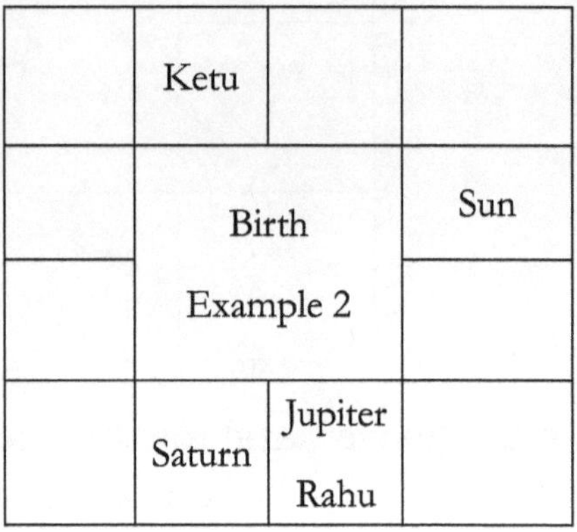

<table>
<tr><td>Ketu</td><td></td><td></td></tr>
<tr><td></td><td rowspan="2">Birth

Example 2</td><td>Sun</td></tr>
<tr><td></td><td></td></tr>
<tr><td></td><td>Saturn</td><td>Jupiter
Rahu</td><td></td></tr>
</table>

	Example 1	Example 2
Jupiter -	252.18°	181.55°
Rahu -	260.45°	182.31°

When the natal Jupiter meets/touches Rahu at first, the children born at that time will have some disability/disorders.

In Example 1, the natal Jupiter is moving towards Rahu. This child could not understand things easily and will be stuttering showing mental retardation. The position of Jupiter pushed the couple to have a child which could not speak normally.

In Example 2, the natal Jupiter touches Rahu at first which was the reason for the couple to have a child unable to walk normally. As Saturn is in the Watery sign and trines to the Sun, it weakened the sperms in the husband which was responsible for the disability.

MISCARRIAGES/ABORTION AND SCORPIO SIGN/RASI

Of all the Signs of the Zodiac, Scorpio is the Sign which gives intensive and severe blemish/maledictions through children and distress/sorrow through them. It does not mean that other Signs/Rasis will not do any harm but its intensity and impact will be comparatively less.

To mention in detail

1. For Scorpions the aspect or conjunction of Mars and Saturn will cause abortion or miscarriage in women.

2. The aspect or conjunction of Mars and Saturn to the 12th house to the ascendant will result in miscarriage and abortion.

3. Presence of more than one inimical planet to Scorpio Sign/Rasi or aspect to Scorpio will cause miscarriage or abortion.

4. Ill-fated children who escape such abortions/ miscarriages suffer disability or some defects.

5. The prevalence of evil scissors misfortune (Placement of two inimical planets on both sides of a bhava/planet} in the 5th Bhavaga in women leads to miscarriage or abortion. A detailed analysis of this position will expose such inimical strength of the planets so placed.

MARRIAGES WITHIN BLOOD-RELATIONS AND PROGENY

This is a sensitive subject which has to be approached with a scientific analysis. When marriages within blood relations are considered the blemish/malefic impact of Mars has to be taken into account.

Blemish/inimical impact of Mars – a clinical Explanation

Rh factor (An indicator of a blood group) is designed after research in monkeys. This refers to genetic inheritance.

In the year 1940, Mr Karl Landsteiner an Austrian-born biologist along with scientist MMrWiener invented the main blood group named as Rh factor. This is one cell part of the blood which can be divided into two.

These two divisions are known as Rh +ve and Rh -ve. The blood which does not have Rh factor is known as Rh -ve and those with Rh factor are known as the Rh +ve group.

A child born to a father with Rh +ve blood group and a mother with Rh -ve blood group will have its blood group as Rh +ve. The blood of the child transfuses with the mother's blood, the +ve or -ve problems occur only after the child's birth. Hence it will not affect the first child.

At the same time...

During the conception of a second child that is formed between a mother who has Rh -ve blood group and a father with Rh +ve blood group, the fetus when in possession of the Rh=ve blood group gets its red cells will be spoiled and damaged by the mother's blood group.

Result of the children born in such conditions

1. The child will have some disability

2. Will have mentally retarded problems (afflicted brain)

3. Might be a special child with a mental disability

Such Rh factors in the blood cells denote the existence of blemish/malediction by Mars.

In the olden days, a good astrologer acted as a good physician and vice versa. Such persons under the guidance, assistance and forethoughts of the Saints and Sadhus gave scientific advice.

With the blessings of my God Shri Ucchishta Maha Ganapathy and if time permits, I would like to write an astrology book based on the terms of scientific facts.

Let us look at the natal (birth) charts of a couple who got married within blood relations and led a wonderful life.

When there existed fear about the birth of a child with a disability for a couple who married within a close blood relation, the remedial aspect of the Mars gave them a healthy child free from disability.

The Husband had an O=ve blood group.

The wife had a B=ve blood group.

		Rahu Jupiter	
	Birth		Moon Saturn
	Husband		
Mercury Mars Sun	Ascendant Ketu Venus		

			Jupiter Rahu
Ascendant	Amsa		
			Mercury Moon
Ketu	Saturn Sun	Mars	Venus

Though Mars is afflicted by its placement in the 2nd house to Scorpio ascendant, as it is the house owned by Jupiter Mars gives a remedial aspect.

The star lord of Mars in Sagittarius is Venus.

The star sub-lord of Mars is Saturn.

Saturn becomes the star lord of the sub-lord Saturn whose star Mars is posited in Sagittarius.

Wife

Her blood group is B+ve. For the Taurus ascendant, Mars is 8th in Sagittarius, though considered a blemish, it is considered a remedial Mars.

The Star lord of Mars is Venus.

The star sub-lord of Mars is the Sun.

<table>
<tr><td></td><td>Venus</td><td>Ketu

Ascendant</td><td></td></tr>
<tr><td>Moon

Mercury

Sun</td><td colspan="2" rowspan="2" align="center">Birth

Rasi</td><td></td></tr>
<tr><td></td><td>Jupiter</td></tr>
<tr><td>Mars</td><td>Rahu</td><td></td><td></td></tr>
</table>

<table>
<tr><td>Moon</td><td>Venus</td><td>Ascendant</td><td>Rahu

Jupiter</td></tr>
<tr><td>Sun

Mercury</td><td colspan="2" rowspan="2" align="center">Amsa</td><td></td></tr>
<tr><td></td><td></td></tr>
<tr><td>Ketu</td><td></td><td></td><td></td></tr>
</table>

The star lord of the sub-lord in which Mars is posited is the Sun.

Here Saturn is the lord of the star in which the sub-lord of Mars is posited for the husband and the Sun is the lord of the star in which the sub-lord of Mars for the wife are conjoined in both the natal (birth) charts of the couple which will not afflict or give any blemish to the child. This rule proves good in almost all horoscopes/natal (birth) charts.

By the Grace of Shri Ucchishta Maha Ganapathy, I intend to do more research on hundreds of such peculiar horoscopes to give fruitful results to this human society.

Natal (birth) chart of a child

The blood group of the child whose natal (birth) chart is given below is A +ve.

The presence of remedial Mars has not affected this child, though the parents had an existence of afflicted Mars blemish.

The child has Mars in the 2nd house to the ascendant. As it is situated in a position giving remedial relief, it has not affected the child.

Ketu	Child		Jupiter
	Rasi/Sign		Saturn Rahu
Moon	Mars Mercury Sun	Ascendant Venus	

Mars			Ketu
Mercury Venus	Amsa		
Rahu	Jupiter Sun		Ascendant

Through the natal (birth) charts both the husband and wife exhibit the existence of the blemish/malediction through children by marrying within blood relations, the child was not affected as their blood groups were different.

Whether the blemish exists or not?

Whenever such doubt arises in the minds of the couple, it is better to do blood tests of both to have a clear mindset.

Sl. No	Gender	Date of Birth/ Time	Place	Blood Group
1	Asokan	29.10.71 -11.45	Rajapalayam	O +ve
2	Mallika	14.10.79 – 10.27	Coimbatore	O +ve
3	Naren	23.04.82 – 17.18	Anaimalai	B +ve
4	Male	22.08.88 – 12.42	Madurai	O +ve
5	Male	18.10.47 – 00.35	Avinasi	B +ve
6	Ramesh	18.04.88 – 09.06	Tirupur	O +ve
7	Srinivasan	05.03.73 – 08.10	Karaikudi	O +ve
8	Velmurugan	21.10.73 – 20.30	Attur	AB +ve
9	Sakthivel	09.10.72 – 10.40	Tirupur	O +ve

In all the above cases the blood group has been confirmed.

To facilitate researchers in astrology, I have given the above details. Our next book on Medical Astrology will have more valuable details and information for Astrologers and Medical professionals who are astrology enthusiasts.

34

MELANCHOLY CAUSED BY THE EARLY DEATH OF VERY YOUNG CHILDREN

Death of children at a very early age within a year of birth causes sorrow to their parents who are unable to revive back to their normal.

Details of a child who died within a year.

Date of Birth: 10.04.1980 Time of Birth: 19.57 Place: Tirupur

Mercury Sun		Venus	
Ketu	Birth		
Moon			Mars Jupiter Rahu Saturn
		Ascendant	

Ascendant – 18.52°

Sun – 27.57°

Moon – 24.05°

Mars – 2.24°

Mercury – 00.52°

Jupiter – 7.03°

Venus – 12.59°

Saturn – 28.02°

Rahu – 2.59°

Ketu – 2.59°

The parents of this child who considered their child heavenly, felt the sorrow of the Universe when it died within a year.

In the natal (birth) chart of the child, for the Movable ascendant Libra, lord of the evil death 11th house Saturn is posited along with Mars in very close degrees to Rahu in the evil house 11th.

Here Mars is the lord of the Maha Dasa (Dasa) establishing the short span of life of the child. More than the position of Mars in the evil 11th house, his status as the Maha Dasa (Dasa) lord of evil death triggered the early death. The planetary alignments are the only reason for the short span of life of the child.

35

TEST-TUBE BABIES AND ASTROLOGY

The Karaka lord for test-tube babies is none other than Rahu who is connected to Jupiter. In the natal (birth) chart of the couples, when Rahu and Jupiter are very strongly connected, they beget test-tube children.

When the planets in transit form the same planetary alignments as in the same planetary alignments in the natal (birth) chart, it fructifies to beget a child.

<table>
<tr><td></td><td></td><td>Sun

Saturn</td><td></td></tr>
<tr><td>Moon</td><td colspan="2" rowspan="2">Birth
Husband</td><td>Ketu</td></tr>
<tr><td>Rahu</td><td></td></tr>
<tr><td>Jupiter</td><td></td><td></td><td></td></tr>
</table>

<table>
<tr><td></td><td></td><td></td><td>Ketu</td></tr>
<tr><td></td><td colspan="2" rowspan="2">Birth
Wife</td><td></td></tr>
<tr><td>Jupiter</td><td></td></tr>
<tr><td>Rahu</td><td>Moon</td><td>Sun</td><td></td></tr>
</table>

Planet	Husband	Wife
Sun	Rohini – 4	Swati - 2
Jupiter	Moolam 4	Sravana – 1 (Tiruvonam 1)
Rahu	Uthrashada – 3 (Uthiradam 3)	Moolam - 4
Ketu	Pushya – 1 (Poosam 1)	Arudra – 1 (Tiruvadhirai 1)
Thithi	Krishna – Ashtami	Shukla - Chaturti

Considering the maintenance of the privacy of the natives, full details were not given here. Researchers can get all/full details from me by contacting me privately or in-person to continue their research. Best wishes to them.

1. In the husband's natal (birth) chart, Rahu is posited adjacent to Jupiter indicating the intensive blemish/malediction through/in having children. This indicates progeny after medication/medical treatment.

2. The Sun + Saturn combination in the natal (birth) chart indicates severe blemish/malediction through children and a deficiency in productive sperm.

3. In the wife's horoscope, Rahu is placed in between Jupiter and Moon projecting a delay in progeny.

4. The Scorpion sign of the wife denotes delay/denying progeny and uterus-related problems.

In the wife's horoscope, Rahu is posited in the sign in which Jupiter is placed in the natal (birth) chart of the husband.

In Wife's horoscope, Jupiter is posited in the sign in which Rahu is plazced in the natal (birth) chart of the husband.

When the couples undertook medical treatment, transit Jupiter was passing over the sign in which Jupiter was posited in the natal (birth) chart of the husband and Rahu in the natal (birth) chart of his wife.

The child was born after medical treatment during the transit of Jupiter and Rahu over the sign in which the natal Jupiter of the husband and natal Rahu of the wife are in their respective natal (birth) charts.

This is a clinical example of the conception and birth of a child artificially (other than naturally) like a test-tube baby or IVF etc during the transit of Jupiter and Rahu over natal Jupiter and Rahu.

The Karaka lord for test-tube babies is none other than Rahu who is connected to Jupiter. In the natal (birth) chart of the couples, when Rahu and Jupiter are very strongly connected, they beget test-tube children.

When the planets in transit form the same planetary alignments as in the same planetary alignments in the natal (birth) chart, it fructifies to beget a child.

Let us examine another set of charts.

<table>
<tr><td>Jupiter

Sun</td><td></td><td></td><td></td></tr>
<tr><td></td><td rowspan="2" colspan="2">Birth

Husband</td><td>Rahu

Mars</td></tr>
<tr><td>Ketu

Saturn</td><td></td></tr>
<tr><td>Moon</td><td></td><td></td><td></td></tr>
</table>

<table>
<tr><td></td><td></td><td></td><td>Moon</td></tr>
<tr><td></td><td rowspan="2" colspan="2">Birth

Wife</td><td>Ketu</td></tr>
<tr><td>Rahu

Mars</td><td></td></tr>
<tr><td></td><td>Jupiter</td><td>Sun</td><td></td></tr>
</table>

Planet	Husband	Wife
Sun	U Bhadrupada - 4 (Uthirattathi-4)	Swati - 1
Jupiter	U Bhadrupada - 1 (Uthirattathi - 1)	Anuradha 2 (Anusham – 2)
Rahu	Uthirashada - 3 (Uthiradam - 3)	Sravana – 1 (Thiruvonam – 1)
Ketu	Pushya - 1 (Poosam - 1)	Pushya – 3 (Poosam – 3)
Thithi	Krishna - Ashtami	Shukla - Chathurthi

When the planets align in the same pattern as that of the natal (birth) chart, it denotes the time to beget a child.

The natal (birth) chart defines the inherited fortunes and the transit of planets during the active period of such fortunes.

Considering the maintenance of the privacy of the natives, full details were not given here. Researchers can get all/full details from me by contacting me privately or in-person to continue their research. Best wishes to them.

1. In the husband's natal (birth) chart, Rahu is posited adjacent to Jupiter indicating the intensive blemish/malediction through/in having children. This indicates progeny after medication/medical treatment.

2. The Sun + Saturn combination in the natal (birth) chart indicates severe blemish/malediction through children and a deficiency in productive sperm.

3. In the wife's horoscope, Jupiter touches Rahu and the Moon touches Ketu at first establishing the presence of severe/intense malediction through children.

4. The Scorpion sign of the wife denotes delay/denying progeny and uterus-related problems.

In the wife's horoscope, Ketu is posited in the sign in which Jupiter is placed in the natal (birth) chart of the husband.

In Wife's horoscope, Jupiter aspect the sign in which Ketu is placed in the natal (birth) chart of the husband.

When the couples undertook medical treatment, transit Jupiter was passing over the sign in which Ketu was posited in the natal (birth) chart of the husband and Rahu in the natal (birth) chart of his wife.

The child was born after medical treatment during the transit of Jupiter and Rahu over the sign in which the natal Jupiter of the husband and natal Rahu of the wife are in their respective natal (birth) charts.

This is a clinical example of the conception and birth of a child artificially (other than naturally) like a test-tube baby or IVF etc during the transit of Jupiter and Rahu over natal Jupiter and Rahu.

<table>
<tr><td></td><td></td><td></td><td></td></tr>
<tr><td></td><td rowspan="2">Birth

Child</td><td>Ketu</td></tr>
<tr><td>Rahu

Jupiter</td><td></td></tr>
<tr><td></td><td></td><td></td><td></td></tr>
</table>

Sign	Wife	Husband	Child
Capricorn	Rahu, Mars	Ketu	Rahu, Jupiter, Sun
Cancer	Ketu, Sun	Rahu, Mars	

Examination of the natal (birth) chart of the child

The child is born during the transit of Jupiter and Rahu over the natal Ketu in the husband's natal (birth) chart and natal Rahu in Wife's natal (birth) chart.

For easy understanding, the relationship between Jupiter, the Sun, Rahu, and Ketu is defined in a tabular form. When transiting Jupiter and Rahu connect to the natal Jupiter and Rahu begetting children artificially like test-tube fructifies.

36

NEGATED TRY FOR A TEST-TUBE BABY

<table>
<tr><td></td><td></td><td>Moon</td><td>Jupiter</td></tr>
<tr><td></td><td colspan="2" rowspan="2">Female

Birth</td><td>Mars</td></tr>
<tr><td></td><td></td></tr>
<tr><td>Chethram</td><td></td><td></td><td></td></tr>
</table>

<table>
<tr><td></td><td>Chethram</td><td></td><td></td></tr>
<tr><td></td><td colspan="2" rowspan="2">Amsa</td><td></td></tr>
<tr><td></td><td></td></tr>
<tr><td></td><td></td><td>Jupiter

Rahu</td><td></td></tr>
</table>

Female Horoscope

Moon's position in degrees	=	48.37
Mars's position in degrees	=	97.45
Jupiter's position in degrees	=	83.19
All the three combined as Chethram in degrees =	241.14

Such computed Chethram 241.14 degrees indicates Sagittarius I part (Moolam). This will be in Sagittarius Sign and Aries Navamsa denoting Male Sign/Rasi and Male Amsa (Navamsa)

This is not fair in female charts. As this fall in Male Sign and Male Navamsa, it indicates issueless stature. She attempted twice to have a test-tube baby but did not materialise.

This can also be computed in a natal (birth) chart way. While both focus on the same result. There are two methods in Prasanna too.

Chethram is computed by adding the position in degrees of Moon, Venus, and ascendant and if this falls in a female sign and female Amsa it indicates that the female is not barren and capable of bearing children making her a complete woman.

If the Chethram in degrees falls in Male Sign and female Amsa, it will not indicate the barren nature of the woman in question, but the existence of some malediction that prevents conceptions. Once some remedial measures are taken up, she can beget children.

Indication of the position of Chethram in Male Sign, Male Amsa (Navamsa)

This position indicates the barren nature of the woman in question who might be facing some blemishes or malediction in having children. This can be construed as a disorder in begetting children in conception.

This Chethram in degrees shall be multiplied by five and divided by 360 to arrive at the point in degrees chosen by the five elements of earth namely 'Pancha bootha Kriya' is indicative of the position of the uterus of the woman.

Notes:

The Chethram in degrees (termed as Chethra sputum) is computed only for female natal (birth) charts

37

IS IT POSSIBLE TO GET A TEST-TUBE BABY?

In the natal (birth) charts that are given below, the Jupiter in Husband's natal chart did not aspect Rahu/Ketu but aspect the Capricorn Ketu in the wife's natal (birth) chart. For the success of artificial insemination/IVF-In Vitro Fertilization, Jupiter should aspect Rahu/Ketu in both natal (birth) charts of the couples. But in the example given below, the rule holds good for only one indicating the failure of the experiment or attempt to have a test-tube baby. Their two attempts did not succeed.

Even during the medical treatment, transit Jupiter did not connect with the natal Rahu/Ketu. In addition to this Saturn is posited in the 5th bhava complicating further delay.

In both natal charts of husband and wife, Saturn is associated/connected with the 2nd Bhavaga. In the wife's natal chart, the 8th house lord Jupiter and the lord of the evil 9th house lord Saturn are conjoined in the 5th house further strengthening the blemish/malediction in having children.

Type 2: Based on Stars/asterisms.

This is calculated based on the star in which a planet is posited giving precise results.

The star in which a planet is posited is presumed as the body.

The star in which the body is positioned becomes life.

The details of the Husband and wife are as follows:

Male: Date of Birth: 08.08.1976 Time: 10.16 a.m. Place: Annur

Female: Date of Birth 21.02.1981 Time 12.16 p.m. Place: Mettupalayam

<table>
<tr><td></td><td>Ketu</td><td>Jupiter</td><td></td></tr>
<tr><td></td><td rowspan="2" colspan="2" style="text-align:center">Husband

Birth</td><td>Sun
Manti
Saturn</td></tr>
<tr><td>Moon</td><td>Mercury
Mars
Venus</td></tr>
<tr><td></td><td>Rahu</td><td>Ascendant</td><td></td></tr>
</table>

<table>
<tr><td></td><td></td><td>Ascendant</td><td></td></tr>
<tr><td>Mercury
Sun
Mars</td><td rowspan="2" colspan="2" style="text-align:center">Wife

Birth</td><td>Rahu</td></tr>
<tr><td>Ketu

Venus</td><td></td></tr>
<tr><td></td><td></td><td></td><td>Saturn
Jupiter
Moon</td></tr>
</table>

Position of 5ᵗʰ lord Saturn for Husband

The 5th lord for Virgo ascendant for Husband becomes Saturn posited in Pushya star is both the body and Jeeva (soul)

(Saturn is posited in Pushya (Poosam) whose star lord is Saturn himself and becomes the Jeevan (soul) or life. The star of the Jeevan (life) becomes Pushya (Poosam) whose lord again is Saturn becoming the body. Both, the body and soul assume full responsibility for the child.

Mercury as the 5ᵗʰ lord for Wife

In the wife's natal {birth) chart, Mercury becomes the lord of the 5th for a wife who is posited in the Star Dhanishta (Avittam) and the lord of the star Dhanishta (Avittam) becomes the Jeevan (soul). The soul Jeevan Mars is posited in Sathabisha

(Sadayam) star owned by Rahu who becomes the body. The planet of the soul Mars is combusted with Sun and also had exchanged his house with Saturn in Virgo.

As the exchange of house and the planet is in retrograde motion he tried out of the means/illegally to beget a child which proved wrong. As the soul of the 5th lord became Rahu/Ketu the blemish and malediction in having children is very severe and strong.

38

LACK OF VITALITY AND BARREN NATURE

A Male and a female may be driven by lust and sexual desires. But only when they do not inherit children or are in a position of impotency or infertility do we term them childless and fail to have descendants. Vitality is not considered a reason for barren nature.

When the 7th house lord and Venus or impacted by eunuch planets, that male becomes impotent and feels infertility.

Venus gains his strength when she is away 7.30° from the Sun and only when he gains strength can the impotency be overcome/averted.

When Eunuch planets Saturn and Mercury conjoin Moon or Venus and gets afflicted, it gives impotency in a male and that too when Venus is close to the Sun and posited within one degree after crossing him. A computation based on the Dwadasamsa (12 divisions of a sign) to distinguish the eunuch's nature is also given. In a male horoscope, if the lord of the 7th house loses or combusts in the planetary war, the native becomes impotent.

This person is now known as transgender but only on a closer look.

<table>
<tr><td></td><td></td><td></td><td></td></tr>
<tr><td>Sun
Jupiter
Mercury
Ascendant
Saturn
Ketu</td><td colspan="2" rowspan="2">Birth

Male</td><td>Mars
Rahu</td></tr>
<tr><td></td></tr>
<tr><td>Venus</td><td>Moon</td><td></td><td></td></tr>
</table>

1. The three Eunuch Planets Saturn, Mercury, and Ketu are posited in Saturn's house Capricorn

2. The planet for vigour is debilitated in Cancer and conjoined with its inimical planet Rahu indicating the weak vigour strength.

3. The 7th house lord responsible inducer of lust/libido Moon is debilitated in Scorpio.

4. In this natal (birth) chart it is good to see the exchange of the 7th lord Moon and the 11th lord Mars. But after an exchange of their houses, they conjoin their inimical and dangerous Rahu, the exchange benefits could not be enjoyed.

5. The lord of the 7th, Vigour and vitality is posited in the 12th house to the house of sexual enjoyment 12th house, indicating the defect in the sexual organ. The parents who were disappointed and sad in the beginning started to hate the child afterwards. Such a bitter feeling or sorrow to parents by the child or hatred feelings of the parents for a child is termed as the blemish/malediction through children.

39

PLANETARY COMBINATIONS THAT DELAY/DENY PROGENY

The Sun + Rahu

In a male natal (birth) chart, if the Sun and Rahu are placed together in a Sign, his sperm cells will be affected. He will be impotent to produce children or will have fewer children.

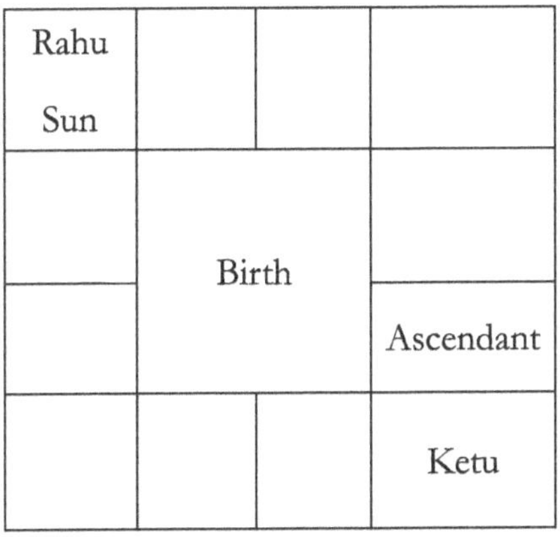

<table>
<tr><td>Rahu
Sun</td><td></td><td></td><td></td></tr>
<tr><td></td><td colspan="2" rowspan="2">Birth</td><td></td></tr>
<tr><td></td><td>Ascendant</td></tr>
<tr><td></td><td></td><td>Ketu</td><td></td></tr>
</table>

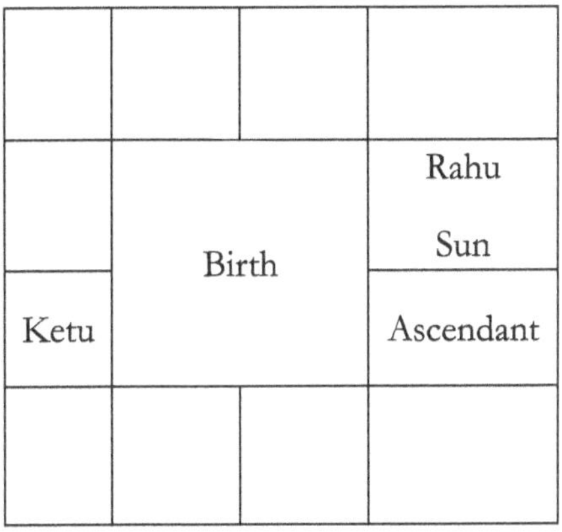

<table>
<tr><td></td><td></td><td></td><td></td></tr>
<tr><td></td><td colspan="2" rowspan="2">Birth</td><td>Rahu
Sun</td></tr>
<tr><td>Ketu</td><td>Ascendant</td></tr>
<tr><td></td><td></td><td></td><td></td></tr>
</table>

In both the horoscopes/natal (birth) charts, Rahu and Sun are posited in the female sign Cancer and Pisces. Both had deficiencies in sperm cells and also had problems in the stomach and spine.

After medical treatment, he had only one child. After Childbirth, the planetary alignments will give severe complications for the father. If the Sun and Rahu are conjoined in the child's natal (birth) chart, the father will get into bad habits.

Rahu's position in the 9th house and the affliction of the 9th lord by Rahu lead to complications and troubles for the father.

Example

<table>
<tr><td>Mars

Manti</td><td>Rahu</td><td></td></tr>
<tr><td rowspan="2"></td><td rowspan="2">Birth</td><td></td></tr>
<tr><td>Ascendant</td></tr>
<tr><td></td><td>Ketu</td><td></td></tr>
</table>

<table>
<tr><td></td><td></td><td></td></tr>
<tr><td>Sun

Ketu</td><td>Birth</td><td>Ascendant

Mars

Rahu</td></tr>
<tr><td></td><td></td><td></td></tr>
</table>

On the day of birth, the child's father died in a fatal vehicle accident.

Notes: Mr Varun Gandhi had a similar planetary combination who lost his father in a tragic accident.

Moon + Rahu

If a child is born with Moon + Rahu combination in its natal (birth) chart, the child would have been born after severe pain. If such children are female babies, they experience the same difficulty during the delivery of their children through severe pain. Such female children experience difficulty throughout their life and through their children. Such children will have obese or very weak and lose the love of either of their parents.

Mars + Rahu/Mars + Ketu

This planetary conjunction gives blood-related problems/deficiencies. Those who have such planetary combinations give birth to reticence/mute/silent children.

40

ADOPTION FORTUNE

1. Adoption status is the result of the denial of progeny to those born in a) Capricorn, Aquarius ascendants ruled by Saturn, b) Gemini, Virgo ascendants ruled by lord Mercury, and c) the houses owned by Saturn and Mercury which becomes the 5th house with Saturn, Manti positioned there which causes the hurdle.

2. Aquarius and Leo's ascendants push towards adoption.

   Why Aquarius and Leo ascendants are listed for adoption?

   While the lords of the 4th house indicate Mother and the 9th house indicates Father the same planet (lord of 4th and 9th houses) who is combusted or severely impacted, it pushes towards adoption as is the case for Aquarius (Venus – lord of 4th and 9th) and Leo (Mars – lord of 4th and 9th).

3. The Bhavaga responsible for adoption is 5th and 8th supported by Saturn and Mercury as Karaka lords.

4. The 5th, 8th, and, 11th bhava lords should not be under combustion in the natal (birth) chart of the person who intends to adopt a child.

Adoption Format:

In the below given example natal (birth) chart 1, the lord of the 5th and 8th house Jupiter is combusted. The 5th and 8th Bhavagas play a responsible role in the adoption and here Jupiter is the lord of both Bhavagas 5th and 8th who is under combustion. As he could not have children by natural method, he adopted two children but both adopted children died causing distress and sorrow to him.

		Ketu	Venus
Mars	Birth		Ascendant
	Female 8-1956		Sun
			Jupiter
	Rahu Saturn		Mercury

The female native had lost all the fortunes bestowed by the 5th Bhavaga. She had a failure in her love affair and when she realised that she could not have a child naturally, she adopted the children.

After the death of the adopted children, she became a poet with abundant imagination.

The positioning of Jupiter and Mars under direct aspect is severe blemish/malediction in having/through children. As the Sun gets the aspect of Mars and Saturn (10th aspect) indicating a deficiency in the strength of the sperms.

The conception is through his 2nd wife after a long wait.

As Jupiter is in the ascendant Kendra and lord of the 5th and 8th houses, he is responsible for adoption. As the 9th house lord of the ascendant and the Karaka lord for children is strong it conferred a child as per rule.

Adoption Format 2

Mahendran Date of Birth: 14.12.1968 – 1.30 a.m.

<table>
<tr><td>Saturn
Rahu</td><td></td><td></td><td></td></tr>
<tr><td></td><td colspan="2" rowspan="2">Mahendran
Birth</td><td></td></tr>
<tr><td>Venus</td><td></td></tr>
<tr><td>Mercury</td><td>Sun</td><td></td><td>Ketu
Ascendant
Jupiter
Moon Mars</td></tr>
</table>

Ascendant	- 17.00
Sun	- 28.29
Moon	- 8.10
Mars	- 27.16
Mercury	- 2.13
Jupiter	- 10.00
Venus	- 11.10
Saturn	- 25.20
Rahu	- 12.09
Ketu	- 12.09

1. The above person to has adopted a child. Here, the lord of the 5th Saturn and lord of the 8th Jupiter are posited in the quadrants (Kendras) exactly 180 degrees apart from each other.

2. In this natal (birth) chart, Ketu is posited in between Jupiter and Mars. Persons with such planetary positions have adopted children.

3. Position of the Sun in trines to Saturn and Rahu causes deficiency in the sperm is our rule which matches and establishes its strength.

4. As per our research rule, the lords of the 5th and 8th are posited in the quadrants (Kendras) to the ascendant and ascendant lord Mercury in this case.

The same position is in his wife's natural (birth) chart which is to be noted for conformity.

Adoption Format 3

Wife of Mr Mahendran Date of Birth 27.05.1977 Time: 13.30

Mars Ketu Venus	Mercury	Sun Jupiter	
	Wife of Mahendran Birth		Saturn
			Moon Ascendant
			Rahu

Ascendant	- 29.04
Sun	- 12.23
Moon	- 25.04
Mars	- 29.08
Mercury	- 17.42
Jupiter	- 18.14
Venus	- 28.14
Saturn	- 18.15
Rahu	- 28.36
Ketu	- 28.36

The above natal (birth) chart is that of a female, the Wife of Mr Mahendran, given earlier.

1. The Rahu posited in the wife's chart is in the attacking position of the Jupiter in Husband's chart.

2. Jupiter and Venus have exchanged their houses. Considering the positions after the exchange, Ketu will be between Mars and Jupiter as in her husband's horoscope.

3. The 5th and 8th lord to the ascendant - Jupiter in this case – is posited in quadrants (Kendras) to the Leo ascendant and the Leo ascendant lord Sun (along with the Sun – 10th house). The same position can be seen in the natal (birth) chart of the husband which is to be noted for conformity.

Adoption Format 4

Dasaradan Date of Birth: 14.12.1968 Time: 1.30 a.m.

	Saturn		Moon
Rahu	Father Birth		Ketu Mars Sun
		Jupiter Manti	Venus Ascendant Mercury

Jupiter Moon			Ketu
Ascendant	Daughter Birth 21.10.2010		
Rahu	Mars	Mercury Sun Venus	Saturn

In the natal (birth) chart of the father, Virgo is the ascendant and the 5th lord is Saturn who is in the debilitated stage in Aries more than this, inimical planets to 5th lord Saturn is posited in the 5th house from Saturn in Aries thus further weakening him and confirming the blemish/malediction in having/through children.

Here a question arises about the aspect of Jupiter on the 5th lord Saturn.

As the lord of evil 7th house Jupiter has conjoined Manti and throws its aspect on Saturn, it has not given beneficial results. As the 5th house lord is positioned in the 8th house this leads to the adoption of a child.

He adopted his sister's child. The Karaka lord Jupiter moves to touch Rahu at first. Jupiter is with Manti here.

The natal chart of the child who is born to a father afflicted by the blemish through children is given above.

Both the 5th house of the father and the ascendant of the girl baby fall in Capricorn. Jupiter in the father's chart is moving towards Rahu and that of the daughter is moving towards Ketu. This indicates the existence of blemish/malediction in children.

Both father and daughter have PUNARPOO misfortune but of a low nature.

The inimical Manti is present in the asterism/star of Rahu for both the father and the daughter which is genetic in nature.

In the father's chart, the lord of the 2nd debilitated Venus is in ascendant and in the daughter's chart lord of the 8th Sun is debilitated in Libra and a quadrant. Both 2nd and 8th are directly opposite Bhavagas.

In the father's natal (birth) chart, Mars is moving towards Ketu and in the daughter's chart Mars moves towards Rahu and both of them have Rahu/Ketu in the 12th house which is a genetic disorder.

41

CONCEPTION APTITUDE BASED ON ASTROLOGY

Conceptional ability can be known based on the point in which the resultant degree by commuting the position of the Sun, Venus and Jupiter and the sign which it occupies. This is known as the degree of conception. if this degree of conception falls in zero/cypher(vacuum) afflicted thithi sign/ Rasi it can be presumed as the chances for begetting children is less. This is done in two ways. A) Based on the natal (birth) chart and B) the Prasanna method. Here, We are going to follow the method based on the natal (birth) chart.

If the total value of the commuted value of the Sun + Venus + Jupiter's position in degrees results over 360 degrees a sum of 360 degrees will be reduced from it. The Original treatises termed this as **BEEJA SPUTUM AND CHETHRA SPUTUM**.

BEEJA SPUTUM

This is computed for Males only through Male natal (birth) charts.

CHETHRA SPUTUM

This is computed in female horoscopes – natal (birth) charts.

COMPUTATION OF BEEJA SPUTUM

This is the resultant degree by adding the position of the Sun + Venus + Jupiter in degrees termed as Beeja Sputum.

If the native's Beeja Sputum in degrees falls in Male Sign, Male Amsa (Navamsa)

This Beeja Sputum degree in Male Sign/Rasi, Male Amsa (Navamsa) indicates that the male is not impotent and capable of begetting children. He is a complete Man with productive ability.

If the native's Beeja Sputum in degrees falls in Male Sign, Female Amsa (Navamsa)

This does not show the impotency of the native but is due to the prevalence of some blemish/curse/malediction in having or through children. The native will have progeny after performing remedies or medical treatment.

If the native's Beeja Sputum in degrees occupies Female Sign, Female Amsa (Navamsa)

This indicates the impotency of the native. This may be due to the existence of a blemish/curse/malediction in having or through children. **In this case, EVEN AFTER PERFORMING REMEDIES AND MEDICAL TREATMENT, THE NATIVE WILL NOT BEGET CHILDREN**.

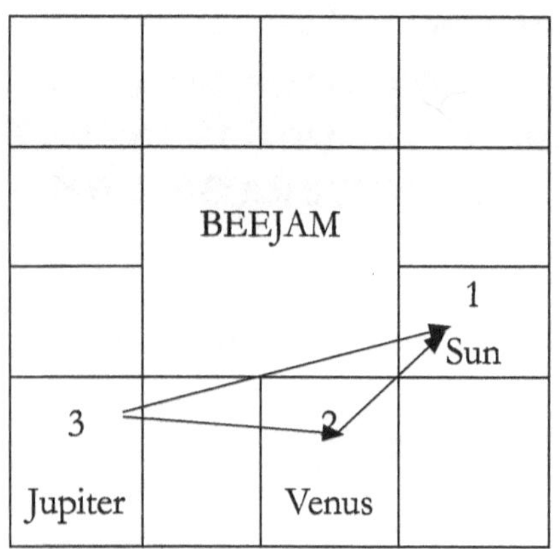

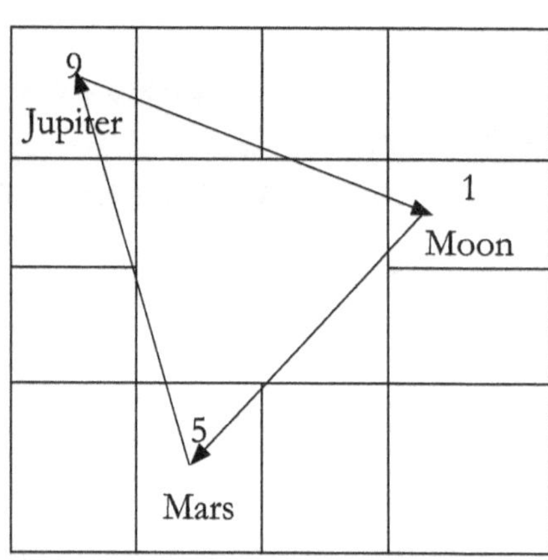

The commuted value of the three Male Sign degrees is termed BEEJAM which helps decide the potency in Males.

The three trine female Sign degrees put together result as CHETHRAM indicating the childbearing capacity in females.

42

HOW TO COMPUTE BEEJA SPUTUM

<table>
<tr><td>Ascendant</td><td></td><td>Sun</td><td>Venus</td></tr>
<tr><td></td><td colspan="2" rowspan="2">Male

Birth</td><td>Jupiter</td></tr>
<tr><td></td><td></td></tr>
<tr><td></td><td></td><td></td><td></td></tr>
</table>

<table>
<tr><td></td><td></td><td></td><td></td></tr>
<tr><td rowspan="2">Jupiter</td><td colspan="2" rowspan="2">Amsa</td><td></td></tr>
<tr><td></td></tr>
<tr><td>Venus</td><td></td><td></td><td>Sun</td></tr>
</table>

Computation of Beeja Sputum

Native's Sun at degrees	- 059.12
Native's Jupiter at degrees	- 113.17
Native's Venus at degrees	- 068.45
The total value of the three planets in degrees	- 241.14

Of this, 240 degrees denotes Scorpio Sign. Hence the balance of 1.14 degrees occupies the star Moolam I part of the Amsa in Sagittarius Sign. Moolam I Part falls in Aries Navamsa which is a Male Sign.

Hence the Beeja Sputum points at Sagittarius Sign which is a Male Sign and Aries Navamsa which is again a Male Sign indicating the full potency of this Native.

This should not be the case in females. This Gentleman tried twice for a test tube baby but did not materialise.

At the outset, it may seem that the ascendant lord is exalted in the 5th house, but the native was more concerned about having children at any cost.

43

HOW TO COMPUTE CHETHRA SPUTUM?

The same position is computed assuming for females. When the position of the Moon, Mars and Jupiter in degrees were added together, the resultant degree will indicate the star position in a sign and corresponding Amsa (Navamsa) position. If the indications are such that the star falls in a female sign and female Amsa, it confers that the female is not barren and capable of conceiving. If the same falls in a male sign and female Amsa, it may not indicate the barren stature of the lady but the existence of some blemish/curse/malediction in having or through children which may fructify after taking remedial measures and medical treatment.

Computation of Chethram Sputum

Native's Moon at degrees - 059.12

Native's Jupiter at degrees - 113.17

Native's Mars at degrees - 068.45

The total value of the three planets in degrees - 241.14

Of this, 240 degrees denotes Scorpio Sign. Hence the balance of 1.14 degrees occupies the star Moolam I part of the Amsa in Sagittarius Sign. Moolam I Part falls in Aries Navamsa which is a Male Sign.

Hence the Chethra Sputum points at the Sagittarius Sign which is a Male Sign and Aries Navamsa which is again a Male Sign indicating the full potency of this Native.

If the Female Native's Chethra Sputum point falls on Male Sign, Male Amsa

This indicates that the lady is barren and not able to conceive. This may be due to the existence of blemish/curse/malediction in having or through children. They could not naturally conceive and can try only artificial/external methods.

44

CONNECTION BETWEEN JUPITER AND SATURN

The proximity of Jupiter and Saturn indicates the existence of the 'Brahma Hathi' blemish/curse. This gives bitterness in the life of children before or after childbirth.

In the below given natal (birth) chart, four planets Jupiter, Saturn, Ketu, and Manti are posited in 15 degrees. Ketu and Manti are placed in trines to Jupiter and Saturn indicating severe blemish/curse/malediction in having/through children.

Date of Birth: 19.02.1981   Time: 13.18   Place of Birth: Coimbatore

<table>
<tr><td colspan="2"></td><td></td><td></td></tr>
<tr><td>Sun
Mars
Mercury</td><td rowspan="2">Female

Birth</td><td rowspan="2"></td><td>Rahu</td></tr>
<tr><td>Ketu
Venus
Manti</td><td>Moon</td></tr>
<tr><td></td><td></td><td>Ascendant</td><td>Jupiter
Saturn</td></tr>
</table>

<table>
<tr><td></td><td></td><td>Ketu
Saturn
Jupiter</td><td>Moon</td></tr>
<tr><td>Mars</td><td rowspan="2">Amsa</td><td></td></tr>
<tr><td>Venus</td><td></td></tr>
<tr><td>Sun</td><td>Rahu</td><td>Mercury</td><td></td></tr>
</table>

Planet	Degrees	Wife
Jupiter	Virgo 15°	In trines to Ketu, and Manti
Saturn	Virgo 15°	In trines to Ketu, and Manti
Ketu	Capricorn 15°	Conjoined Ketu and Manti
Manti	Capricorn 15°	Conjoined Ketu and Manti

Here, Jupiter and Saturn are in the same 15 degrees and the position of Saturn alongside the Karaka for Child, Jupiter is considered as severe/intense malediction.

Such placements of Jupiter and Saturn in close degrees are termed as 'Brahma Hathi' blemish

The proximity of Jupiter and Saturn indicates the existence of the 'Brahma Hathi' blemish/curse. This gives bitterness in the life of children before or after childbirth.

Ketu and Manti are positioned exactly at the same degrees in trines to Jupiter establishing the blemish.

In Navamsa's 6th house, Jupiter, Ketu, Saturn, and Manti confirm that her First husband remains childless.

TO DECIDE ON TRANSIT RESULTS

To decide on the year of the event, the Annual planets Jupiter and Saturn should be considered.

To decide on the month of the event, the monthly planets Mars and the Sun should be considered.

To decide on the day of the event, the daily moving Moon has to be reckoned with.

To decide on the exact time in hours, the ascendant has to be calculated.

The lords of the Maha Dasa (Dasa), and Anthar Dasa (Bukthi) will be closely connected with the lord of the 5th Bhavaga.

The years should be calculated based on Jupiter.

The Month should be calculated based on the Sun.

The days should be calculated based on the Moon.

Any event will be complete only when the Maha Dasa (Dasa) and Anthar Dasa (Bukthi) are connected with the transit of the planets.

Below given are the natal (birth) charts of three Past Prime Ministers of India.

Natal (birth) chart pf Pt. Jawaharlal Nehru

Cancer ascendant whose 5th lord is Mars. According to our rule, only when the annual planets Jupiter or Saturn or both aspects of the 5th lord or the 5th house the native will beget children.

<table>
<tr><td></td><td></td><td></td><td>Rahu</td></tr>
<tr><td></td><td rowspan="2" colspan="2" align="center">Pt. Nehru

Birth</td><td>Moon
Ascendant</td></tr>
<tr><td></td><td>Saturn</td></tr>
<tr><td>Jupiter
Ketu</td><td>Sun</td><td>Venus
Mercury</td><td>Mars</td></tr>
</table>

His daughter Mrs Indira Gandhi was born when the transit Saturn aspects the natal Mars through its 3rd aspect and the transit Jupiter's 5th aspect of natal Mars.

The natal (birth) chart of Mrs Indira Gandhi is given below.

<table>
<tr><td></td><td></td><td>Jupiter</td><td>Ketu</td></tr>
<tr><td></td><td rowspan="2" colspan="2" align="center">Mrs Indira

Gandhi

Birth</td><td>Ascendant
Saturn</td></tr>
<tr><td>Moon</td><td>Mars</td></tr>
<tr><td>Venus
Rahu</td><td>Sun
Mercury</td><td></td><td></td></tr>
</table>

In this natal (birth) chart, when transit Saturn in Gemini threw its 3rd aspect on natal (birth) 5th house lord Mars and

Another annual Planet Jupiter during its transit in Sagittarius aspect the 5th house lord (posited in Leo) by its 9th aspect Mr. Rajiv Gandhi born.

The natal (birth) chart of Mr. Rajiv Gandhi

			Saturn
Ketu	Mr. Rajiv Gandhi Birth		
			Ascendant Moon Rahu
Jupiter			Mars

The Natal (birth) chart of a father:

In the below given natal (birth) chart, during the transit of the annual planet Saturn in Gemini threw its 10th aspect of Jupiter, 5th house of Scorpion ascendant (Pisces) and the 2nd house Sagittarius Jupiter.

The transit Saturn is indicated separately.

Example:

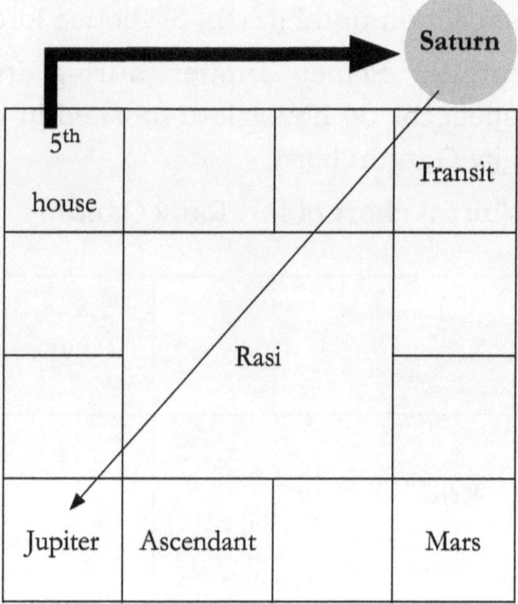

Another Example

	5th house		
	Father		
	Birth		
Ascendant			Mars 5th Lord

This is the natal (chart) of a person who has two sons. Let us examine this chart.

As per this Sagittarius ascendant, the 5th house is Aries and its lord Mars becomes the 5th house lord who is in Virgo. During the transit of Saturn in Pisces, its aspect was on Mars.

At the same time, transits Jupiter's aspect to the 5th house Aries through its 9th aspect. Hence both the annual planets have aspected the 5th house and 5th house lord confirming progeny to the native.

Saturn			
	First Son Birth		
			Jupiter

	Saturn		
Rahu	Second Son Birth		
			Ketu
		Jupiter	

As per the father's horoscope, the birth period of the 2nd son can be computed in two ways.

Method 1

As per the father's natal (birth) chart, the 5th house is Aries and its lord is Mars. In Aries, the annual planet Saturn is posited and another annual planet Jupiter aspects the 5th place giving the fortune of his 2nd child through the aspect of two annual planets over the 5th house.

Method 2

As per the rule for the 2nd child, the Bhavaga for his father (Sagittarius ascendant) 7th house is Gemini. Accordingly, the transit Saturn aspect Gemini through its 3rd aspect and the transit Jupiter aspect Gemini through its 9th aspect confirm the birth of his second son.

46

MAHA DASA (DASA), ANTHAR DASA (BUKTHI) LORDS AND CHILD BIRTH

When the lords of the trines of the ascendant are connected as the Maha Dasa (Dasa), and AntharDasa (Bukthi) of the native, marriage or childbirth takes place.

Date of Birth of the native: 22.08.1956 Time: 10.30 a. m Place: Tirupur

<table>
<tr><td></td><td></td><td>Ketu</td><td>Venus</td></tr>
<tr><td>Moon
Mars</td><td colspan="2" rowspan="2">Father
Birth</td><td></td></tr>
<tr><td></td><td>Jupiter
Sun</td></tr>
<tr><td></td><td>Rahu
Saturn</td><td>Ascendant</td><td>Mercury</td></tr>
</table>

<table>
<tr><td></td><td></td><td></td><td></td></tr>
<tr><td>Rahu</td><td colspan="2" rowspan="2">Child
Birth</td><td></td></tr>
<tr><td></td><td>Jupiter</td></tr>
<tr><td></td><td></td><td></td><td>Saturn</td></tr>
</table>

Fifth Bhavaga Lord	: Saturn
Planet in the Fifth Bhavaga	: Moon
Lord of the 11th House	: Sun
Planet in the 11th house	: Sun, Jupiter

The above are responsible Planets for the birth of a child.

These positional planets will be the lords of the Maha Dasa (Dasa), and Anthar Dasa (Bukthi) during childbirth.

Kindly note the Maha Dasa (Dasa), and Anthar Dasa (Bukthi) are currently in operation during childbirth.

During the birth of the First child, the native was running Saturn Maha Dasa (Dasa), Moon Anthar Dasa (Bukthi), and Jupiter Prithyanthar Dasa (Anthram).

The Maha Dasa lord Saturn is the lord of the 5th house.

Anthar Dasa (Bukthi) lord Moon is in the 5th house Aquarius.

The Prithyanthar Dasa (Anthram) lord Jupiter is in the 11th house Leo.

During the birth of his 2nd son, the native was running Saturn Maha Dasa (Dasa), Jupiter Anthar Dasa (Bukthi), and Sun Prithyanthar Dasa (Anthram).

The lord of the 5th house Saturn is in the 2nd house.

The Anthar Dasa (Bukthi) lord Jupiter is in the 11th house.

The Prithyanthar Dasa(Anthram) lord Sun is in the 11th house.

Every event will be associated with the lords of the Maha Dasa (Dasa), Anthar Dasa (Bukthi), and Prithyanthar Dasa (Anthram) with related Bhavagas and transit.

The lord of the 5th house is Aquarius and its lord is Saturn who is posited in the 2nd house Scorpio. Transit Saturn aspect the 5[th]lord through its 3rd aspect and transit Jupiter aspect the 5th house through its 7th aspect.

47

TRANSIT AND CHILDBIRTH

Duration of time birth based on the transit of planets.

Research Rule 1

When the transit Jupiter or Saturn aspect the lord of the 5th or 5th house it will be the time of birth of a child.

Research Rule 2

If in a natal (birth) chart, Rahu or Ketu is posited in the 5th house, the child will be born when transiting Jupiter or transit Saturn aspect the 5th house wherein the Rahu or Ketu is posited.

This rule proved to be successful in 90%of the cases.

The Maha Dasa (Dasa), and Anthar Dasa (Bukthi) will be connected to childbirth and the mishap will be when they do not align together.

Research Rule 3

It can be made sure that without any connection between transit planets Jupiter and Saturn to natal Jupiter or the lord of the 5th or the 5th Bhavaga, there will be no possibility for the birth of a child.

When practised in the right way, this rule will fetch a good name and fame for consultant astrologers.

The transit position of planets during the birth of the child

Lord	Planet	Transit	Maha Dasa (Dasa), Anthar Dasa (Bukthi)
2nd house Lord	Mars	8th house	Anthar Dasa (Bukthi)
Planet Lord in 2nd house	Saturn	2nd house	PrithyantharDasa (Anthram)
Jupiter	In 11th house	In the star of Maha Dasa (Dasa) Lord	The aspect of 5th house

Notes:

The Rasi/Sign of the Zodiac is different from the Bhavaga. When Maha Dasa (Dasa) and Anthar Dasa (Bukthi) are considered only the Bhavaga positions of the planets are to be reckoned. The date of birth of the child is considered the eventual transit time.

A Simple note to my Co-astrologers:

The deep study and analytical skill in transit knowledge alone help the astrologers to get name and fame through their predictions. This is true. I admire and follow the words/spells of my preceptors/Gurus as more powerful than the Master of Archery the Great Arjuna in Mahabharata. Hence the blessings and tireless training in transit elevate you to greater heights and I wish you success.

48

CHILDBIRTH AND RELATED DISEASES

Female baby date of Birth: 29.01.1981 Time of Birth: 14.07 Place: Coimbatore

Manti		Ascendant	
Mercury	Rasi/Sign		Rahu
Ketu Mars Sun			
Venus		Moon	Saturn Jupiter

		Sun Saturn	Jupiter Moon Ketu
	Amsa		
			Ascendant
Rahu Venus	Manti Mercury		Mars

This female is well-educated and possesses good character.

1. She had a uterine cyst.

2. She had high PH in her blood for which she has been taking continuous treatment due to which she remains childless so far.

Notes:

PH is a scientific character which possesses acidity and alkalinity in the blood.

Let us now look at the astrological factors for this PH prevalence.

Reason:

The first sign to have a severe blemish in having/through children is Scorpio and next comes the sign Libra.

To be more precise, the star Visakam exhibits the blemish through children. In addition to this, the 3rd aspect of Saturn is over Scorpio.

Added to this is the presence of an acidic-natured planet Ketu is associated with the two hot planets, Mars and the Sun in which exalted Mars adds salt to the wound.

Planetary alignments in Amsa (Navamsa)

In Navamsa the combination of the Sun and Saturn alongside Jupiter + Ketu, and Moon + Ketu leads to complications in the uterus. The position of combined Sun and Saturn in trines to Mars triggers the presence of high PH in blood.

In Amsa, the placement of the Sun + Mars combination in trines to Saturn as in the Sing/Rasi is the important reason for the presence of a high PH factor in the blood.

Saturn in Virgo has exchanged its house with Mercury in Aquarius pushing the native to try for a test tube baby.

As Saturn and Jupiter are posited in the same degrees and Saturn exchanged house with Mercury, the artificial insemination method of conception through the husband's sperm failed.

They got a child through other means. Let us look at the natal (chart) of the husband.

The natal (birth) chart of the Husband- Year of Birth 1976

Birth of the child – September 2004

<table>
<tr><td></td><td>Ketu</td><td></td><td></td></tr>
<tr><td rowspan="2"></td><td rowspan="2" colspan="2">Husband

Birth</td><td>Saturn</td></tr>
<tr><td></td></tr>
<tr><td></td><td></td><td>Rahu</td><td></td></tr>
</table>

<table>
<tr><td></td><td>Rahu</td><td></td><td></td></tr>
<tr><td rowspan="2"></td><td rowspan="2" colspan="2">Child
Birth
Period</td><td>Saturn</td></tr>
<tr><td></td></tr>
<tr><td></td><td></td><td>Ketu</td><td>Jupiter</td></tr>
</table>

When this chart is compared with that of his wife given above, it can be seen that the natal Rahu of the husband is over the natal Moon in the wife'

The placements of the planets here can be compared with the rules given under Chapter 20 – 'PLANETARY PARENTHESIS IN COUPLES'

49

DO I HAVE PROGENY?

If an aspirant raises the question about his entitlement of having a child through 'Prasanna', a 'Prasanna Chakra' has to be designed/drawn and accordingly its results have to be declared. If the same question is asked in general terms, his Karmic results about having progeny should be determined based on his/her natal (birth) chart and then the approximate time of childbirth can be revealed.

To evaluate whether one is entitled to have progeny/inheritance of children, the native's ascendant lord should be posited in the 2nd, 5th, or 11th house or the Maha Dasa (Dasa), Anthar Dasa (Bukthi)nor the lords of 2nd, 5th, or 11th house or the planets posited in should be in operation. If it is not the currency of the operation of such Maha Dasa (Dasa) or Anthar Dasa (Bukthi) it can be declared that the native is not fortunate to have progeny/descendants.

When the native does not have the good fortune to have children, further analysis should not be done.

The Bhavaga indicators of a child are 2nd, 5th, and 11th.

The Bhavaga that prohibits/deny progeny/descendants is the 4th and 10th.

A new entrant to the family and presence in the family is indicated by the 2nd Bhavaga.

The Bhavaga indicator of a couple is their 5th.

The 11th Bhavaga indicate a desirable/happy event.

Hence it is vital to consider the 2nd, 5th, and 11th Bhavagas to decide about progeny/having children/descendants.

50

TRANSIT AND CHILDBIRTH

Date of Birth: 05-03-1973   Time: 08-30a.m.   Place: Karaikudi

<table>
<tr><td>Ascendant</td><td></td><td>Saturn</td><td>Ketu</td></tr>
<tr><td rowspan="2"></td><td rowspan="2" colspan="2">Male

Birth</td><td rowspan="2"></td></tr>
<tr></tr>
<tr><td>Jupiter</td></tr>
<tr><td>Rahu

Mars</td><td></td><td></td><td></td></tr>
</table>

<table>
<tr><td>Jupiter
Venus
Mercury</td><td>Saturn</td><td></td><td></td></tr>
<tr><td>Sun</td><td rowspan="2">Transit
07.03.1999
17.30</td><td>Rahu</td></tr>
<tr><td></td><td>Ascendant</td></tr>
<tr><td></td><td></td><td>Moon
Mars</td><td></td></tr>
</table>

The lord of the 2nd Bhavaga was running the Maha Dasa (Dasa)

The lord of the 2nd is the Anthar Dasa (Bukthi) lord

The Planet in the 2nd house (at the birth of the father) is the Prithyanthar lord (Anthram)

The child was born during the above planetary combination.

The native was running Saturn Maha Dasa (Dasa), Mars AntharDasa (Bukthi) and Saturn Prithyanthar Dasa (Anthram). The child was born when the Maha Dasa (Dasa), Prithyanthar Dasa (Anthram) Dasa was transiting over Aries, the 2nd house to his natal ascendant and Anthar Dasa (Bukthi) lord Mars aspect Aries, the 2nd house to the natal ascendant Pisces.

Even a malefic planet will perform the event when it is related to the Bhavaga but will indicate that there will be some distress connected to the event.

The transit Jupiter is posited in the asterism of the Maha Dasa (Dasa) lord Saturn in Uthra Bhadra.

51

SEPARATION IN THE FAMILY AFTER CHILDBIRTH

It is a deadly sin to blame the child if something goes wrong after conception due to the difference of opinion leading to separation among couples or quarrels/fights between them.

The planetary alignments or combinations of such couples who blame the child will be as under:

1. Saturn + Rahu
2. Saturn + Ketu
3. Mars + Rahu
4. Mars + Ketu
5. The Moon + Rahu
6. The Moon + Ketu
7. Venus + Rahu
8. Venus + Ketu
9. The Sun + Rahu
10. The Sun + Ketu

Whichever the ascendant be, the prevalence of one or more than one such planetary combination alignments, the couple's part from each other and blames the child/children.

These planetary alignments/combinations/associations will work for any ascendant.

Example:

Saturn Rahu		Ascendant	
	Husband Birth		
			Mars Ketu

Mars Rahu	Wife Birth		
		Ketu Venus	

In the husband's natal (birth) chart, planetary alignments leading to separation from the wife after conception are present.

1. Saturn + Rahu
2. Mars + Ketu

In the wife's natal (birth) chart separation from husband indicators after conception are present.

1. Mars + Rahu

2. Venus + Ketu

Both husband and wife led their life fighting each other after the birth of the child.

Notes:

Those born in Aquarius will see their parents living in separation, if they have Mars posited in 6th house Cancer, For Aquarius ascendant, the 4th house lord is Venus and for Venus, the Kalathra Karaka/Karaka for the life partner is Mars who debilitates in Cancer, the 6th house for Aquarius indicating the loss of affection of either of the parents.

	3rd house stepmother	Mother	
Ascendant	Example Horoscope 1		Mars
	10th house stepfather	Father	

	Father	10th house Stepfather	
		Example Horoscope 2	Mars
			Ascendant
	Mother	Venus 3rd house Stepmother	

In Example chart 1, the 12th house lord to the 4th house Taurus for Aquarius ascendant representing mother and 2nd house Scorpio to 9th house representing Father is the same Mars is debilitated in Cancer. For Aquarius and Leo ascendants, malefic and afflicted weak Mars affects the native to have a stepmother or stepfather.

Example Chart 1 had debilitated Mars in Cancer for Aquarius ascendant forced the native to have a stepmother. In Example 2 chart, debilitated Mars in the 12th house to Leo ascendant pressed the native to live under the care of a stepfather.

SOUL (JEEVA) AND BODY (SHARIR) METHOD

This is an old treatise to judge progeny in two methods.

Method 1: Based on Sign/Rasi

Method 2: Based on Stars/asterisms.

Method 1: Based on Sign/Rasi

According to Kalapurusha (Time personified) philosophy 5th house lord the Sun is designated as the body (Sharir). The lord of the Sign/Rasi in which the 5th house lord according to the birth ascendant posited is considered as the soul (Jeeva).

Rahu	Saturn		
Sun Mercury Ascendant	Birth 9.3.1969		
			Jupiter Ketu

In the above natal (birth) chart, the 5th house lord to the ascendant based on Kalapurusha (Time personified) is the Sun is the body of a child and accordingly in this case, the Sun is posited in Aquarius spotting its lord Saturn as the body of the Sun.

According to the birth ascendant, the Sign/Rasi lord in which the 5th lord is posited becomes the soul and in this case for the Aquarius ascendant the 5th house lord is Mercury and as Mercury is posited in Aquarius itself, its lord Saturn becomes the soul for Mercury.

As per the above computation of the lord of the Soul- body both are the same who is Saturn in this case. The strength and weakness of the Soul and body lord decide the progeny. Debilitated Soul and body lord deny and affects progeny severely. Here debilitated Saturn in Aries denies progeny to the native.

The above native undertook many tests and tried many means of medical treatments including In Vitro fertilization (IVF) methods and test tube babies which did not fructify. The couple remains childless till now.

Example:

Ascendant	Ketu	Jupiter	
			Saturn
	Husband Birth		
Moon			Sun
	Rahu		

		Ascendant	
			Rahu
Ketu Sun Mercury	Wife Birth		
			Jupiter Saturn

In the case of the husband, the body of the Sun – the Sun himself as he is in Leo.

As Moon is the 5th house lord for Pisces ascendant and posited in Capricorn, the lord of Capricorn Saturn becomes the Soul- Jeeva. But the Sun and Saturn are posited in a 2/12 position between themselves establishing severe delay in having children.

In the wife's natal (birth) chart, the body becomes Saturn (the Sun in Capricorn) and the soul too becomes Saturn as the 5th lord to ascendant is Mercury posited in Capricorn. Here Saturn is in retrograde motion.

As Saturn is the lord of both Jeeva and Sharir (Soul and body) for both husband and wife, it indicates delayed progeny. In the case of the husband, Saturn has exchanged its house with the lord of the 5th moon and retrograde in the wife's natal chart reducing the possibilities of progeny to the couple.

53

PROGENY AS PER SOUL (JEEVA) AND BODY (SHARIR) RULE

Female: Date of Birth: 04.01.1984 Time: 03.30 a.m. Place of birth: Coimbatore

Male: Date of Birth: 19.08.1976 Time: 09.30 p.m. Place of Birth: Kodaikanal

<table>
<tr><td></td><td></td><td>Rahu</td><td></td></tr>
<tr><td></td><td colspan="2" rowspan="2">Birth

Female</td><td></td></tr>
<tr><td></td><td></td></tr>
<tr><td>Moon
Sun
Mercury
Jupiter</td><td>Ketu
Venus
Ascendant</td><td>Saturn
Mars</td><td></td></tr>
</table>

<table>
<tr><td>Ascendant</td><td>Ketu</td><td>Jupiter</td><td></td></tr>
<tr><td rowspan="2"></td><td colspan="2" rowspan="2">Birth

Male</td><td>Saturn</td></tr>
<tr><td>Sun
Venus
Mercury</td></tr>
<tr><td></td><td></td><td>Rahu</td><td>Mars</td></tr>
</table>

Soul (Jeeva) and Body (Sharir) Rule based on Sign

As per Kalapurusha (Time personified) philosophy 5th lord the Sun and the 5th lord to Scorpio ascendant Jupiter both are posited in Jupiter's house Sagittarius declaring Jupiter as the Soul (Jeeva) and Body (Sharir) lord.

As per the female native's chart, Jupiter becomes the lord of the Soul and body which is in the star of Ketu and posited exactly 60 degrees apart from Saturn who throws his 3rd aspect. This position confirms that begetting a child will be delayed.

As per the rule of Conception immediately after marriage will result in disability to the child, the child is premature. Jupiter is posited exactly 60 degrees apart from Saturn.

As per our research rule Mars and Saturn are conjoined in the 12th house which is the 8th house to the 5th house, the indicator of progeny. This status indicates severe disease in the first child or complications in the delivery to the female native.

54

WHAT IS MEANT BY SAPTAMSA CHAKRA (SEVENTH DIVISIONAL CHART)?

Saptamsam is the division of a Sign into seven parts. A Planet's beginning Sapthamsa starts from the Sign in which it is posited.

When the Sign consisting of 30 degrees is divided into 12 parts each 2.5 degrees is called Dwadasamsam.

Each Dwadasamsam lasts 2.5 degrees,

This delineation describes the progeny, and the good and bad the native is going to face through them.

The aspect of Jupiter and Saturn on the 5th house of the Sapthamsa ascendant will reveal begetting children.

In the delineated chart of the Saptamsa, when powerful Mars is posited in trines or quadrants to the Sun, the native had only male children or more male children with almost nil or one girl babies.

Similarly, in the delineated Saptamsa chart, when the ascendant and the Moon fall apart in the male signs, the native beget more male children or only male children giving almost nil or limited.

Male: Date of Birth: 20.04.1975 Place: Dharapuram

The blood group of the native: A+ve

In XY chromosomes only 20% (twenty) will have masculine anatomy/characters and

80% (Eighty) will have feminine character/anatomy prevalent as per medical journals/bulletins.

Jupiter	Sun Mercury	Ketu Venus	Saturn
Mars	Male		Moon
	Birth		
	Rahu Ascendant		

	Moon Mars	Mercury Sun	Ascendant
Venus	Saptamsam		
Jupiter		Saturn	

The progeny is exhibited by the delineation of the Saptamsa chart and in this, the ascendant falls on Gemini in a Male sign.

The first child is indicated by the 5th Bhavaga which is a male sign here. The Second child is indicated by the 7th Bhavaga, a male sign and the third by the 9th Bhavaga. Which is again a male sign.

The native had all three children as female babies only. When the Saptamsa signs indicated all as male signs, the babies born were all girl babies.

In such horoscopes/natal (birth) charts, if the baby born is a male, all the others follow suit. Similarly, if the firstborn baby is a girl, the rest of the babies will also be of the same gender. As Saturn and Venus have changed their houses, the native is very fond of a male boy. As the indicators of the Saptamsa points are in male signs but when the results are the opposite, the desire to have a child of the opposite sex is more.

According to our rule of indications to have more male babies, the need for male planets Mars, Jupiter, and the Sun to be in trines to the Sun has not happened here. Jupiter is in the 8th house to the Sun and Mars standing against the wish of the native to have a male child.

Notes:

Does the natal (birth) chart of the male native decide the birth of a male or female baby? Certainly not. The birth of a child is decided by the native chart of the female only. This can be very clearly seen in my medical astrology book.

The native is born in Aslesha (Ayilyam) star and he came for a consultation with me on a day when the ruling star was the same Aslesha (Ayilyam). He undertook his first medical treatment on a day when the Moon was passing over Revathy star. His Second medical test was conducted when the star was on Jyeshta (Kettai) and again he met me on a day when the Jyeshta (Kettai) star was ruling. He undertook his third medical examination on a day when Revathi was the star.

Hence, he consulted me mostly on days when the stars of Mercury were predominantly ruling the days of consultation. To keep the client's privacy in check, I could not share the full details here.

Here my co-astrologers should note about the role of Mercury and its stars and their hidden agenda to reveal something else that drives the native. Here only the almighty can lead us.

Birth of a female: 1981   Blood Group: A +ve

	Female		Rahu
Ketu	Birth		Mars
Venus	Sun Moon Mercury	Jupiter	Saturn Ascendant

		Ascendant Moon Mercury	Venus
Mars			Ketu Sun
Rahu	Saptamsam		Saturn
	Jupiter		

In Sapthamsa, the position of male planets Sun, Mars, and Jupiter in trines- Quadrants (Kendras)the native will inherit more male children, else it will be female babies. According to our above rule, here Mars is posited in the 8th (Ashtama) house to the Sun, it has not conferred fortunes to have a male baby even though Jupiter is placed in trines to the Sun. He was blessed with four female babies.

Male: Date of Birth: 18.10 .1947 Time: 00.35 Place of Birth: Avinasi

The Blood group of the native is B +ve

In XY chromosomes only 20% (twenty) will have masculine anatomy/characters and

80% (Eighty) will have feminine character/anatomy prevalent as per medical journals/bulletins.

Even at his 56th year of Age he has no deficiency in haemoglobin but has a high level in it.

	Rahu		
	Male Birth		Mars Saturn Ascendant
Ketu Moon Jupiter	Venus Mercury Sun		

Mercury	Mars	Ketu	Jupiter
Ascendant			Saturn
	Saptamsam		Moon
Venus	Rahu	Sun	

Saptamsam denotes progeny/having children. In this horoscope, the Saptamsa ascendant of the native is Aquarius which is a male sign.

The 5th Bhavaga indicates the first child, the 7th Bhavaga by the 2nd child and the 3rd child is indicated by the 9th Bhavaga. In this case, all three 5th, 7th, and 9th Bhavaga are male signs.

This native was blessed with three male children.

In this Saptamsa chart, all the Bhavagas denoted only male signs giving birth to male babies. As per our rules of placement of male Planets the Sun, Mars, and Jupiter in Kendras (Quadrants) or trines to the Sun the native inherited male children (Mercury has exchanged houses with Jupiter and occupies the 5th house – a trine- after an exchange of houses. His wife had conceived four times of which three times she delivered male babies and one resulted in a miscarriage.

As Mars and Jupiter are posited in trines and Kendras (Quadrants) to the Sun, it indicates only male babies.

DWADASAMSA AND PARENTS

The Upagrahas or satellites to the main Planets do play a vital part in the birth of children. And that too 'Shodasa Varga' which depicts 16 different types of charts for different delineations to judge the strength of different Bhavagas is too important whenever some doubts arise in the minds of the astrologer in arriving at the results. Of this, the Dwadasamsa chakra or chart helps in knowing the status of the parents. It indicates the status of parenthood of the native.

What is Dwadasamsa Chakra or Chart?

A Sign or Rasi of 30 degrees is subdivided into 12 parts each accounting for 2.5 degrees termed as Dwadasamsam. The beginning of Dwadasamsa begins from the Sign from where the planet is posited extending to 2.5 degrees.

How to judge the results of Dwadasamsa?

If the Sun, who represents father, will not be on good terms with his children when he is posited in the 6th, 8th, or 12th place from the Dwadasamsa ascendant.

Similarly, the father and his children will not be against each other if the lord of the 9th to the Dwadasamsa ascendant is hidden in the 6th, 8th, or 12th.

Placement of the 9th lord or the Sun in the 6th, 8th, or 12th house to the Dwadasamsa ascendant and if an eclipse (lunar or Solar) takes place on that day of birth, it causes severe misunderstandings and enmity with the father. The status of the father will be in the worst stage and during the currency of bad Maha Dasa (Dasa), Anthar Dasa (Bukthi) in operation may bring death to the father.

Who is responsible for the blemish in progeny/not having children...

In the materialistic life, understanding between husband and wife including sexual union is most important to lead a happy peaceful life for the family and children. Let us examine the role of the blemish in having children through physical/sexual union among couples.

When the 5th house to the Dwadasamsa ascendant indicates an odd sign and the lord of that odd sign is posited in odd Sign/Rasi, *then the husband is responsible* **for the blemish to take its effect in not having children.**

When the 5th house to the Dwadasamsa ascendant indicates an even sign and the lord of that odd sign is posited in an even Sign/Rasi, *then the wife is responsible* **for the blemish to take its effect in not having children.**

When the 5th house to the Dwadasamsa ascendant indicates an odd sign *and the lord of that odd sign is posited in an even Sign/Rasi, then the wife is responsible for the blemish* **to take its effect in not having children. The Vitality or Vigour of the Husband is subdued/reduced.**

If all the three eunuch planets, Saturn, Ketu, and Mercury are present in the 7th house to the 5th lord of Dwadasamsa ascendant, either of the couples (Husband or Wife) will be a eunuch/impotent which renders the physical/sexual union a void to remain childless.

In female natal (birth) charts, if Moon is posited in the 7th house to Dwadamsa ascendant and gets the aspect of Saturn, there will be a problem in the uterus for female natives. This rule proves right to be successful in 85% of cases.

Likewise, In female natal (birth) charts, if Saturn is posited in the Dwadasamsa ascendant and Moon is stationed in 7th to it, there to Uterus related problems prevail in female natives.

In the below given natal (birth) charts of two women, the Moon is placed in the 7th house to the retrograde Saturn in Dwadasamsa ascendant.

	Ascendant Saturn		
	Female chart		Mars
	Dwadasamsa		
Jupiter		Moon	

Jupiter Ascendant Mercury	Saturn		
	Female chart		
	Dwadasamsa		
			Moon

In both the natal (birth) charts, Jupiter and Saturn are in Retrograde motion. There were pregnancy-related problems for which the treatment was not successful.

Laparoscopic surgery was done in the uterus and continuous treatment is being undertaken. Both the husbands of the female natives were cleared of any clinical deficiency. In such cases, Dwadasamsa is useful in the assessment of who has the deficiency among the couples.

Notes:

If Moon and Mercury are combined in any sign in Dwadasamsa, the native's father will have extra-marital relations and may be living with another woman/concubine. If the same combination of Moon and Mercury is found in any quadrant (Kendra) or trines, the native's father will be living with another woman/concubine in public.

If the same conjunction of Moon and Mercury is seen in hidden places of 6th, 8th, or 12th the native's father will be having extramarital affairs and will lead a secret life.

When the Sun is posited in the 2nd house to Dwadasamsa ascendant, the native may have to live in separation from his/her father. Had the same period of death (Maraka) as the father, the separation will be due to the death of the father. The period of evil will give the separation due to distress, sorrow and losses. The Sun and the Moon in trines in Dwadasamsa exhibit that both the parents are united together.

The placement of the Sun and the Moon in 6th and 8th places within themselves indicates that the parents live apart.

The powerful 4th lord in Dwadasamsa indicates that both parents have a long life.

The above results are more than 80% appropriate and successful in practical life in natal (birth) charts.

Example:

<table>
<tr><td></td><td>Ascendant

Mars</td><td>Sun</td><td></td><td></td><td></td><td>Mars</td><td></td><td></td></tr>
<tr><td></td><td rowspan="2" colspan="2">Dwadasamsa 1</td><td></td><td>Moon

Mercury</td><td rowspan="2" colspan="2">Dwadasamsa 2</td><td>Ketu</td></tr>
<tr><td></td><td></td><td></td><td>Sun</td></tr>
<tr><td></td><td>Moon

Mercury</td><td>Jupiter</td><td></td><td></td><td>Ascendant</td><td></td><td>Saturn</td></tr>
</table>

In Chart 1, Moon and Mercury are conjoined and in quadrant (Kendra) 7th house to the Aries ascendant. The native's father was living with another woman as husband and wife for a long time.

In Chart number 2, Moon and Mercury are conjoined and, in a quadrant, (Kendra) 4th house to the ascendant. As Mercury had exchanged houses with Saturn he lived with another woman as husband and wife for some time and parted from her.

CHILDREN AND DISEASES

When the Star lord or the Sign lord of the Child is combusted or debilitated, it shows chronic diseases in the child.

<table>
<tr><td></td><td></td><td></td><td>Ketu
Moon</td></tr>
<tr><td rowspan="2"></td><td rowspan="2" colspan="2">Birth 1</td><td>Mars</td></tr>
<tr><td></td></tr>
<tr><td>Ascendant</td><td></td></tr>
<tr><td>Rahu</td><td></td><td></td><td></td></tr>
</table>

<table>
<tr><td></td><td></td><td></td><td></td></tr>
<tr><td rowspan="2"></td><td rowspan="2" colspan="2">Birth 2</td><td>Ketu</td></tr>
<tr><td rowspan="2">Ascendant</td></tr>
<tr><td>Rahu
Moon</td></tr>
<tr><td></td><td></td><td>Sun</td><td></td></tr>
</table>

In Example 1, the child is born in Mrigasira star and the star lord Mars is debilitated. This child suffered from nervous problems.

In Example 2, the child is born in Uthrashada (Uthiradam) and the star lord is debilitated in Libra. The child is born blind.

TRANSIT AND CHILD HEALTH

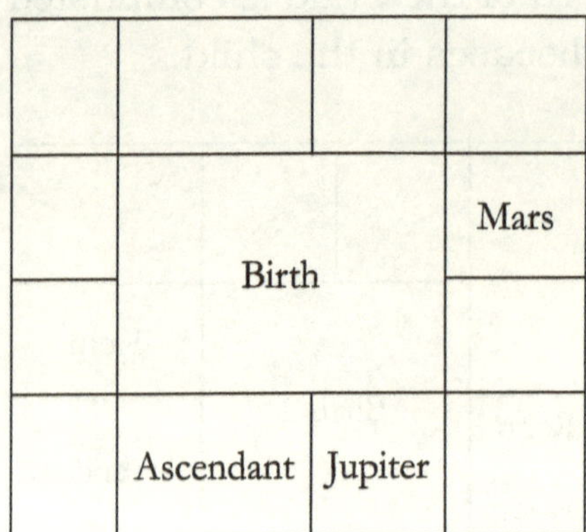

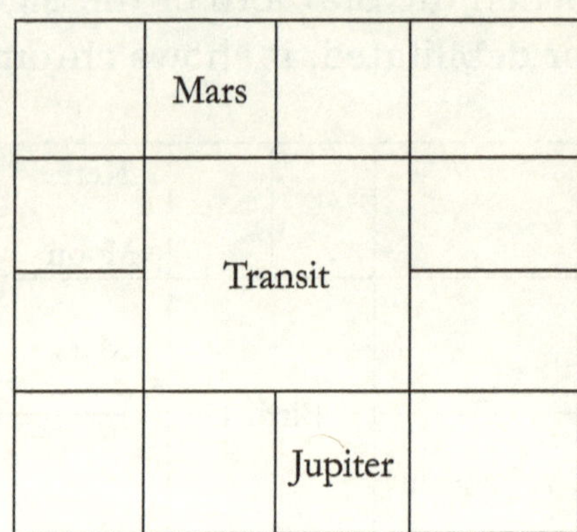

In the above natal (birth) chart of the child, for Scorpio ascendant Jupiter is posited in the Chitra star owned by the 6th lord of diseases, Mars for Scorpio ascendant. The 4th aspect of Mars from Cancer is on Jupiter, thus connecting the lord of the diseases with the lord of the 5th house.

During the transit of combined Jupiter and Mars, the child was severely affected. The lord of the 6th Mars is in the 6th house Aries and transit Jupiter is in the star of the 6th lord. This transit establishes the effect of planetary alignments in the natal (birth) chart.

MAHA DASA (DASA) LORD AND THE CHILD

Example: 1

<table>
<tr><td></td><td>Saturn</td><td></td><td></td></tr>
<tr><td></td><td rowspan="2" colspan="2">Father
Birth</td><td>Ketu</td></tr>
<tr><td>Rahu

Mars</td><td></td></tr>
<tr><td></td><td></td><td></td><td></td></tr>
</table>

<table>
<tr><td></td><td>Ketu</td><td></td><td></td></tr>
<tr><td>Ascendant

Saturn</td><td rowspan="2" colspan="2">Child
Birth

6.11.1994</td><td>Mars</td></tr>
<tr><td></td><td></td></tr>
<tr><td></td><td>Jupiter

Moon</td><td>Rahu</td><td></td></tr>
</table>

The native was running Saturn Maha Dasa (Dasa), Ketu Anthar Dasa (Bukthi), and Mars Prithyanthar Dasa (Anthram). His child was born in Aquarius ascendant, Scorpion Sign/ Rasi, Jyeshta (Kettai) star, and on a Sunday.

The child was born in Aquarius ascendant, one of the two zodiac signs of the Maha Dasa lord Saturn. In the father's natal (birth) chart, the lord responsible for the child Ketu was in Aslesha (Ayilyam) star owned by Mercury and another star Jyeshta (Kettai) of Mercury has become the birth star of the child. Scorpio the sign of the Prithyanthar Dasa (Anthram) lord Mars is the birth sign of the Child.

The star of the Anthar Dasa (Bukthi) lord Ketu Makam is aspected by the Maha Dasa lord Saturn.

The child was born when the Maha Dasa lord Saturn of the father is in Aquarius, Anthar Dasa lord Ketu in Aries, and Prithyanthar Dasa lord Mars in Aslesha star in Cancer which can be seen in the birth chart.

Notes:

The child was born to execute the Karmic results of the father based on other planetary alignments. How can this be distinguished as the blemish to the parents by the birth of the child? A child is born according to the Maha Dasa (Dasa), Anthar Dasa (Bukthi) currently in operation and the transit of planets. When this is analyzed from different angles more clarifications will be known.

Example 2

			Ketu
	Mother	Jupiter	
	Birth		
Rahu			

		Child	Moon
		Birth	
Ascendant			

During the birth of the child, the mother was running Rahu Maha Dasa (Dasa), Jupiter Anthar Dasa and Rahu were in Sagittarius and Jupiter in Cancer. Her child was Born in Sagittarius ascendant and Punarvasu star (Punarpoosam) Cancer, the ascendant being the Maha Dasa lord Rahu's position and Anthar Dasa (Bukthi) lord Jupiter's position as the Sign Cancer.

The child's ascendant lord, Rasi/Sign lord and Star lords are that of the mother's Maha Dasa (Dasa), and Anthar Dasa (Bukthi) lords establishing the Karma relativity theory according to other Planets.

Example 3

During the birth of the child, the father was running Saturn Maha Dasa(Dasa), Mars Anthar Dasa (Bukthi), and Jupiter Prithyanthar Dasa (Anthram).

His child is born in Libra ascendant, and Scorpion Sign/ Rasi in Anuradha Star (Anusham) which In the father's natal (birth) chart indicates the Maha Dasa lord Saturn as Star-lord Saturn and Anthar Dasa lord as the Sign lord Mars and the Sign lord where the Dasa lord posited (Taurus in father's natal chart) has become the ascendant lord (Venus of Libra). It is a clear indication that the Karma of the father is reflected in the child's birth chart by planetary alignments as per the chart given below.

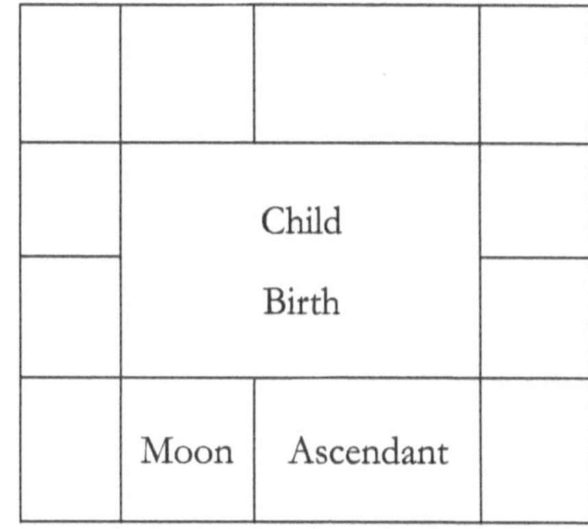

Example 4

Below given is my assistant Mr. Velmurugan's birth chart along with his child.

He was running Venus Maha Dasa (Dasa) and his Venus is posited in Scorpio. His child is born in Barani Star owned by Venus in Aries.

<table>
<tr><td></td><td></td><td></td><td></td></tr>
<tr><td></td><td rowspan="2" colspan="2">Velmurugan

Birth</td><td></td></tr>
<tr><td></td><td></td></tr>
<tr><td></td><td>Venus</td><td></td><td></td></tr>
</table>

<table>
<tr><td></td><td>Moon</td><td></td><td></td></tr>
<tr><td></td><td rowspan="2" colspan="2">Child

Birth</td><td></td></tr>
<tr><td></td><td></td></tr>
<tr><td>Ascendant</td><td></td><td></td><td></td></tr>
</table>

The Current Maha Dasa (Dasa) lord Venus and the Sign/ Rasi lord where he was posited have become the Star-lord (Barani- Venus) and the Rasi/Sign lord (Moon in Aries- Mars) establishing the execution of father's Karma through other planets according to the birth chart of the child.

CONCEPTION AND SEXUALLY TRANSMITTED DISEASES

Couples desirous of having children pass the blame on the other when they are unable to have children. An analysis of the 'Shodasamsa Varga Chakra' or the 16th part analysis will give the result about who is at fault. In the 'Shodamsa or D16 divisional chart', if the 7th lord of the ascendant has conjoined Saturn or Venus or gets their aspect and at the same time the 6th lord is posited in the houses of Saturn, Venus, or Moon, the native will be suffering from sexually transmitted diseases.

This may also be one of the reasons for the denial of progeny/not having children. The 'Shodasamsa or D16 divisional chart' refers to the pleasure derived by a person.

REMARRIAGE FOR THE SAKE OF BEGETTING CHILDREN

It requires extraordinary astrological talent, knowledge, wisdom and God's grace to declare inheritance/progeny of children only through remarriage when the first wife is still alive. With half-cock knowledge, an astrologer should not attempt at separating the family in the name of inheritance of children through second/remarriage.

Many dejected people approach me with the question of remarriage for begetting children. I have scolded them at times and advised them to have patience or alternative methods. For the question of the availability of an alternative in such cases, the answer is 'Yes' and the result is through 'YAMAKANDA SPUTUM'.

HOW TO COMPUTE THE 'YAMA KANDA SPUTUM'?

Sl. No	Day	Degrees to be added for Day time	Degrees to be added for Night time
1	Sunday	108	312
2	Monday	84	288
3	Tuesday	60	264
4	Wednesday	36	240
5	Thursday	12	216
6	Friday	156	192
7	Saturday	132	336

The 'Yama Kanda Sputum' for a particular day and time can be derived by adding 'The Sun's position in degrees on that particular day + the degrees for daytime/Night time for that particular day.

Result:

If the result after adding the 'Yama Kanda sputum (degrees)' and 'ascendant sputum (degrees)' denotes the Dual or Upaua Sign/Rasi, the native will beget children through his first wife only after marrying multiple times. It is important to note that there is no mention that the Second or third wife will conceive.

This can only be correctly predicted by an expert in astrology and Prasanna with the Grace of God. While such predictions are made there should be no greed in the minds of the astrologer.

JUPITER AND MOON COMBINATION

The Fortune or Misfortune exhibited by the combination/conjunction of Jupiter and the Moon can be declared only after thorough research. At the same time, I can very strongly and boldly say that the combination/conjunction of Jupiter and the Moon gives threatening evil results and never fail in it.

The conjunction/combination of Jupiter and the Moon or their aspect on each other gives one of the following results. Such conjunction/combination in the 7th house gives delay/denial and hurdles in progeny/having children and problems through them.

1. Delays or Denies progeny.
2. Pushes the native into poverty after the birth of the children thereby forcing them to hate living.
3. Makes nursing children difficult.
4. Children will be grown/up under the care of somebody else thereby reducing the mutual affection between the parents and the children.
5. Children will revolt/act against the father.
6. Extends hardcore blemish/difficulties through children.
7. Causes life in exile/underground/absconding for some days or months or some years.

Example:

Late Chief Minister Dr M. G. Ramachandran's natal (birth) chart is a typical example of this rule as the ascendant is Virgo and Jupiter along with the Moon is in Pisces.

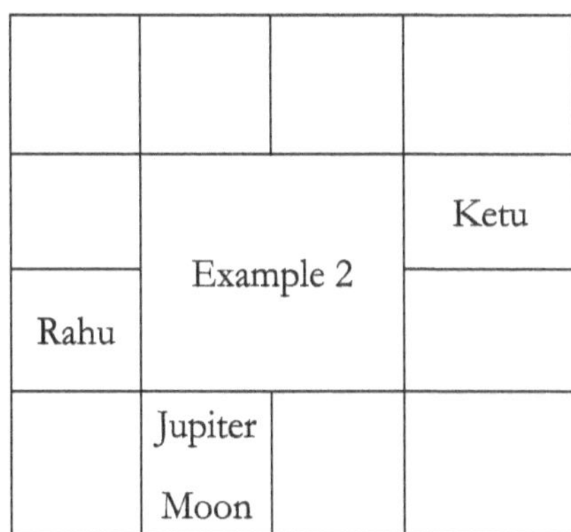

In example 1, after the birth of the child, the parents suffered from poverty forcing the child to grow under its grandmother's care. The child did not respect his father to the extent he respects his grandparents.

Example 2

In the above example, the child has Jupiter + Moon combination in Scorpio. This child is living with their mother from the day of birth and does not know the love and affection of his father.

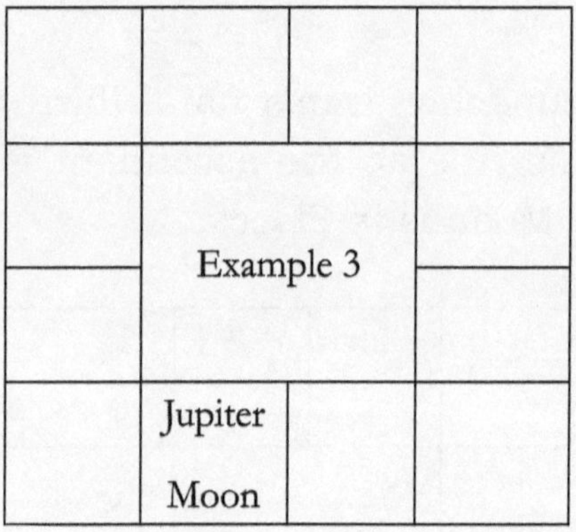

	Example 3		
	Jupiter Moon		

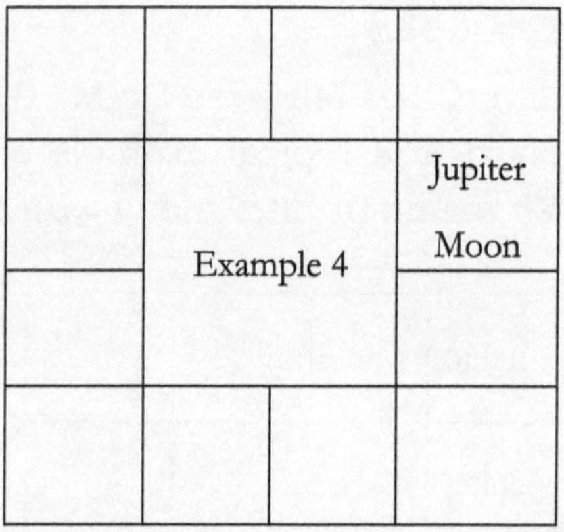

			Jupiter Moon
	Example 4		

In example 3, Jupiter and the Moon are Scorpio and from the day of its birth, it is being grown in its maternal uncle. The parents of the child are living overseas and the child does not know what is real love and affection of parents are.

As it is grown in a maternal uncle's house, it is more affectionate towards its mother than its father.

Example 4

In the above case, the conjunction of Jupiter and the Moon is in Cancer. From the day of his birth, the child is living with his mother and stepfather not knowing the love and affection of his real father. As he is grown in his mother's guard, he did not show even a per cent of love towards his stepfather. His mother is the sole reason for their separation as she moved out of the house with her beau after the birth of the child. When his real father met him, he was twenty years of age. How to term this fate as?

63

SOME IMPORTANT DEGREES RELATED TO PROGENY (CHILDBIRTH)

Calculations:

YAMA KANDA SPUTUM (DEGREES)

To know this the relative degrees for the Day should be known.

YAMA KANDA SPUTUM – IN PRASANNA METHOD

Yama Kanda Sputum = (Native's current day Agas/30 x days' time {Ghatis})

SUTRA (RULE) TO KNOW THE SANTANA SUN DEGREES

Five times the ascendant position in degrees is termed as SANTANA SUN DEGREES which can be used for judging the results through a natal (birth) chart and the 'PRASANNA' method.

Example

Assume Ascendant degree as 20. Multiply by 5. 20 x 5 = 100 degrees

SUTRA (RULE) TO KNOW THE SANTANA MOON DEGREES

Five times the Moon's position in degrees is termed as SANTANA MOON DEGREES which can be used for judging the results through a natal (birth) chart and the 'PRASANNA' method.

Example

Moon's position = 80 degrees x 5 = 400 degrees – 360 degrees as more than one cycle = 40 degrees.

THIS PORTION WILL BE DISCUSSED IN DETAIL IN THE NEXT PART OF THIS BOOK.

SANTANA THITHI

Beneficial aspects of Santana thithi:

Does it help in knowing whether the fortune of having children is there? If so, what kind of child will it be? How many children? Will they be free from malediction and be fortunate?

Santana thithi answers such types of questions.

How to compute 'Santana thithi'?

When Santana Moon Degrees are deducted from Santana Sun degrees and the sum is divided by 12 the resultant is the Santana thithi.

Rule:

Santana Sun degrees – Santana Moon degrees / 12 = Santana thithi.

Example:

Santana Moon's degrees = 40 degrees

Santana Sun's degrees   = 100 degrees

(100) – (40) = 60 / 12 = 5 Santana thithi degrees.

YOGA SPUTUM AND BEGETTING CHILDREN

The Yoga sputa are arrived at by adding the ascendant degrees and Yama Kanda degrees.

The anger and Curse of God, unfulfilled submissions to God will result as a blemish and this can be known when eunuch planets Saturn, Mercury, and Ketu are present in the 9th Sign/Rasi from Yoga sputa conjoined or aspect by luminaires the Sun or the Moon.

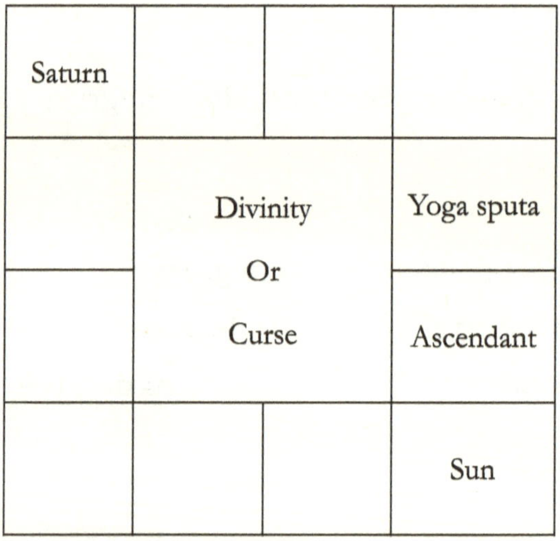

Saturn			
	Divinity Or Curse		Yoga sputa
			Ascendant
			Sun

If Manti is present in the stars of luminaires the Sun or the Moon in the 6th Sign/Rasi from the Yoga sputa and receives the aspect of eunuch planets Saturn, Mercury, or Ketu, then it is Blackmagic or voodoo initiated by opponents not to beget children/blemish not to have children. (It is one of the various types of Black magic).

Example:

As per our research, Manti is present in the Sravana (Thiruvonam) star which belongs to the Moon and receives the aspect of one of the eunuch planets Saturn's 3rd aspect.

	Blackmagic		
Manti			Yoga sputa
	Saturn		

The native of this horoscope says that his opponents have initiated some Blackmagic/voodoo against him because of which he has no children. According to our research rules, this chart proves to be the right example.

To know the existence/initiation of Blackmagic, the 'Prasanna' is the easy and right way.

The connection between the ascendant lord, evil lord and 6th lord confirms the presence of Blackmagic.

66

CHATHURSPUTAM AND BEGETTING CHILDREN

Chatursputam is arrived at by adding the degrees of the ascendant, the Moon, Yama Kanda, and Manti positions.

If the total exceeds 360 degrees, then 360 degrees should be deducted from it. The resultant point of degrees is named Chathursputam and when that point of degrees falls on an odd sign and odd Navamsa (Amsa) positioned in quadrants (Kendras) and trines to Jupiter, it assures progeny or begetting children for sure.

If the Chathursputam point is in an odd Sign, odd Navamsa but the eunuch planets Saturn, Mercury, and Ketu are positioned in trines to Jupiter it denies progeny and the native will not get children.

If the Chathursputam point falls on an even sign and an even Navamsa but is not stationed in the Kendras (Quadrants) or trines then too the native is denied of progeny and the native will not get children.

Example:

Ascendant sputa   =   10.12°   Aries

The Moon Sputa   =   80.25°   Gemini

Yama Kanda Sputa =   25.10°   Aries

Manti Sputa   =   125.52° Leo

Adding all these four together, the resultant point degrees is 241.39° indicating 1st Part of the Moola star in Sagittarius Sign/Rasi.

	Yama Kanda Jupiter Ascendant		Moon
	Confirmed Progeny?		
			Manti
Chathur sputa			

Chathur sputum is situated in Sagittarius under the 9th aspect of Jupiter. As per our research, the native faced severe hurdles in begetting children and development of the child and finally had a child.

	Mars Ascendant		Moon
	Confirmed Progeny?		
			Manti
Chathur sputum Saturn Jupiter			

Jupiter is in Sagittarius along with Saturn where the Chathur sputum is present. As per our research rule, he will face a hard delay in progeny and even after initial problems did not get children as not only Jupiter but eunuch planet Saturn is also posited along with Jupiter where Chathur sputum is denying the progeny.

67

FUTURE STATUS OF THE ADOPTED CHILD

In the case of adoption, a question will arise as to whether the adopted child will take care of the adopted Parents in future for which the adoption degree point will give the perfect answer.

The adoption degrees are arrived at by adding the position in degrees of the lord of the 12th and the position in degrees of Jupiter.

If malefic planets Saturn, Mars, Rahu, or Ketu are posited in the 12th house to the adoption degree, they are denied, progeny.

<table>
<tr><td></td><td></td><td></td><td></td></tr>
<tr><td></td><td rowspan="2">Confirmed

Progeny?</td><td></td></tr>
<tr><td>Manti</td><td></td></tr>
<tr><td></td><td></td><td>Adoption

Degrees</td><td>Mars

Saturn</td></tr>
</table>

In the example chart, the adoption degrees computed by adding the lord of the 12th and Jupiter falls in Libra Sign and to its 12th house Virgo, malefic Mars and Saturn are posited denying adoption fortune to the native.

This native is not fortunate to have an adopted child.

LINEAGE POSITION IN DEGREES

By adding the Yama Kanda degrees with that of Manti's position in degrees, the Lineage position in degrees can be arrived at. If this lineage point becomes 3rd, 5th, or 7th position from the Birth star of husband or wife they are denied of any lineage and do not have progeny.

Manti is posited at 125.52° and the Birth star of the husband is Visaka.

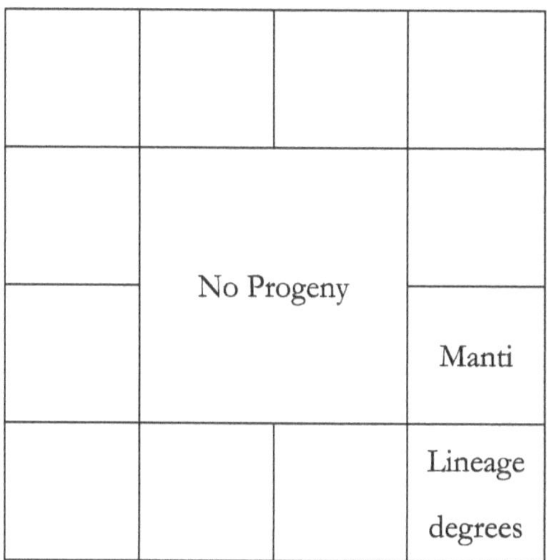

For the wife, the lineage point degree falls in Virgo, Uttara Phalguna (Uthiram) star. The 5th star Visakam from this becomes the Birth star of the Husband showing no compatibility.

As the husband is not in a position to beget children naturally, he can choose the artificial way of getting children and look for an (egg) donor.

WILL THE ADOPTED CHILD BE GOOD?

The point of adoption will be the resultant degrees obtained by adding ascendant degrees and Yama Kanda degrees. If that point falls in Mercury's house and the lords of siblings Mercury and Mars aspect them (Example chart 1), **then two children may be adopted or go for adoption twice**.

Mars	Example 1		
			Mercury Adoption degrees

	Example 2		
			Sun Mercury Adoption degrees

In Example 2, the adoption point degrees in Virgo are conjoined by the Sun and Mercury. Such a combination of the Sun and Mercury or their aspect on the adoption point degrees makes the adopted child turn against the adopted family or be sub-standard/degraded.

Saturn and Mercury are responsible for adoption- both to give and get. But when they become the lords of the adoption point degrees (lord of the star belonging to the degrees) or gain positional strength in the ascendant, they deny the fortune of adoption. Such denial or misfortunes will be negated if either Jupiter or Venus conjoin or aspect the adoption point degrees making the adopted children come good.

PREGNANCY POINTS IN DEGREES

To know the Pregnancy ascendant

The Pregnancy ascendant lord is the lord of the Sign in which the Pregnancy point of degrees falls arrived by adding the ascendant degrees + Moon's position in degrees + Manti's position in degrees + Yama Kanda point in degrees. The Pregnancy ascendant indicates the status of growth of the embryo to the fetus stage. A good position of the Pregnancy ascendant and the Moon indicates that the mother and the child are safe.

When the Moon is not well positioned, but the pregnancy ascendant is good states that the child inside the womb is safe but the mother's status is not.

If the Moon is well positioned and the pregnancy ascendant is not so good, it shows that the status of the child and its growth is not in order but the mother is in good condition. Such pregnancy conditions are to be seen using 'Prasanna' after pregnancy and before childbirth.

The 7th house from the pregnancy ascendant and the Sun will convey about the father of the child. While 'Prasanna' methods are adopted, it has to be seen in different ways before childbirth and after childbirth. The prayers through 'Pregnancy Prasanna' before childbirth indicates the 7th house as that of the father and after childbirth, the natal (birth) chart of the child indicates the 9th house (3rd house to 7th house) about the father.

PERPETUAL PROGENY POSITION IN DEGREES

This is the balance degrees after adding the Moon's position in degrees+ to the Sun's position in degrees and dividing it by a star's position in degrees (13.20°).

Is Progeny possible after doing remedies?

When couples approach the astrologer to know about their progeny possibilities, the transit Moon should pass over apa Jaya sthanas (the houses next to Upa Jaya sthanas) for the husband and in Upa Jaya sthanas (known as the 3rd, 6th, 10th, and 11th houses) for wife, any remedial measures undertaken will fructify. Otherwise, it will not materialise.

As far as the begetting of children, the remedial measures shall be undertaken only if no physical ailments are there. If those ailments can be cured through the intake of medicines and treatment, it should be attempted before opting for remedies as remedial measures will not work when the physical conditions are bad.

On the day of consultation for progeny, only if the Moon passes over the Upa Jaya sthans 3rd, 6th, 10th, and 11th houses in the woman's horoscope (wife's), the benefits/results should be declared.

Healthy Pregnancy points in degrees

In a woman's natal (birth) chart, the beginning point of the 5th bhavaga in degrees, lord of the 5th house in degrees, Jupiter's position in degrees should be added together and from the sum, the Moon's position in degrees should be deducted. The resultant degrees are termed Healthy Pregnancy points in degrees.

In a woman's horoscope, her sexual desires/interest in the conjugal union should be measured by the strength of Venus, her desire/interest in pregnancy by the strength of Mars, and her capabilities to conceive by the strength of the Moon.

Number of Pregnancies?

The 3rd house, the lord of the 3rd house, and the Navamsa (Amsa) of the 3rd house lord decide the number of pregnancies and means of pregnancies.

Is there a fortune to have children?

The 5th house lord, the 5th house, the planet in the 5th house, and the Planet in the asterisms/star of the 5th house lord reveal whether a couple has the fortune of begetting children.

Of this, if there is a benefic planet posited in the star of the 5th house lord, then the couples are sure to get children.

72

EFFECTS OF JOINT HOROSCOPES (NATAL CHARTS)

What is meant by joint effects?

The combined effects of a planet in a particular Bhavagam in a horoscope when matched to another horoscope (natal chart) in the same Bhavagam and the planet posited in it.

Explanation:

Let us suppose that a planet is in Cancer of a natal chart. The effect it causes in another chart with the planet posited in Cancer is termed a joint effect.

If Jupiter is posited in a Sign of a native and the same sign as Rahu/Ketu is posited in another native's chart, it causes some impacts and it is termed as blemish through/in having children. And the position of Rahu/Ketu in higher degrees than that of Jupiter is considered to be a very severe blemish/curse in having children/progeny.

Example:

Husband: Date of Birth: 29.12.1962   Wife: 1970

Jupiter	Husband		
Moon Saturn	Birth		
Sun Manti			

Rahu	Wife		
Mercury	Birth		Ketu
	Jupiter		

In the wife's natal (birth) chart, Rahu is posited in Aquarius whereas Jupiter is posited in the husband's natal (birth) chart. This is a severe blemish and causes a denial of progeny and distress/sorrow in having/through children.

If Rahu/Ketu is posited in the Sign/Rasi of one's natal (birth) chart in which the other's 5th house lord is positioned causes severe blemish/distress in having/through children.

If in a couple's natal (birth)charts, if the 5th lord is placed in a Sign/Rasi wherein the other's Mars is placed, then the progeny-related problems can be cured through medical treatment. If Manti is placed instead of Mars, then it can be set right through remedial measures.

In a couple's natal (birth) chart, the 5th lord should be weak which means the 5th lord should not be debilitated, combusted or conjoined with Rahu/Ketu.

Placement of Jupiter's inimical planet in the Sign/Rasi of one of the couples in which Jupiter of the other is positioned indicating the blemish/distress/sorrow in having/through children.

Positioning of a combusted planet or Manti in one of the couples Sign/Rasi in which the 5th lord of the other is placed will also lead to distress/blemish through/in having children.

73

JOINT EFFECTS OF JUPITER AND MANTI

Husband: 24.11.1970/11.09   Wife: 09.02.1974/14.29

<table>
<tr><td></td><td>Saturn®</td><td></td><td></td></tr>
<tr><td>Rahu
Manti</td><td rowspan="2">Husband

Birth</td><td></td></tr>
<tr><td>Ascendant</td><td>Ketu</td></tr>
<tr><td></td><td>Jupiter
Venus®</td><td></td></tr>
</table>

<table>
<tr><td></td><td></td><td>Ascendant
Ketu
Saturn®</td></tr>
<tr><td>Jupiter</td><td rowspan="2">Wife

Birth</td><td></td></tr>
<tr><td>Venus®</td><td>Moon</td></tr>
<tr><td>Rahu</td><td></td><td></td></tr>
</table>

Sl. No	Husband	Wife
1	Manti 326.05°	Jupiter 300.02°
2	Rahu 304.30°	Rahu 242.20°
3	Saturn®	Saturn ®
4	Venus®	Venus®
5	Lords of 2nd & 5th in Retrograde Motion	Lords of 5th & 8th in Retrograde Motion

1. Rahu and Manti are posited in Aquarius Sign in Husband's natal (birth) chart While Jupiter is posited in Aquarius in the wife's natal (birth) chart. It resulted in

miscarriages even after many times of conceptions. She remains childless so far.

If Rahu/Ketu is placed in higher degrees than Jupiter's position, then it denotes the prevalence of high blemish/curse in having children. This position is seen here.

2. In both charts lord of the 5th is in Retrograde motion.

3. In both the natal (birth) charts Saturn and Venus are in Retrograde motion.

In the natal charts of women who have Rahu/Ketu in the ascendant experience problems in the fallopian tube. And in this woman's case, natal Ketu of her husband is over her natal Moon confirming the problems related to the fallopian tube. They are under medical care for parenting.

Notes:

1. Jupiter + Rahu + Manti

2. Jupiter + Ketu + Manti

3. Jupiter + Rahu + Sun

4. Moon + Rahu + Jupiter

5. Moon + Rahu + Jupiter's aspect

6. Moon + Ketu + Jupiter

7. Moon + Ketu + Jupiter's aspect

All the above Planetary combinations/alignments will face bad omens. Turmeric mixed with salt water will restrict/remove such bad omens.

74

BEGETTING ONLY GIRL BABIES

1. When the 5th house becomes Jupiter's Sagittarius or Pisces and Jupiter is posited in female sign in all Varga Chakras (Delineation Charts).

2. 5th house falls in a female Sign and female Planets Venus, Moon, or Mercury in it.

3. 5th house lord is present in a female Sign and female Stars.

4. When Saturn is strongly connected to Rahu/Ketu

   Then this position only bestows girl babies.

Example: 1

			Jupiter (Pushya)
	Birth		
	Example1		
	Ascendant		

Ascendant Mars			
			Jupiter (Pushya)
	Birth		
	Example 2		
			Moon (Hastham)

In example 1, the 5th house is a female Sign (Pisces) and its lord Jupiter is posited in Cancer, another female Sign.

Example: 2

The Pisces ascendant lord Jupiter is in the female Sign Cancer. The 5th house Cancer is a female Sign and its lord Moon is in another female Sign Virgo in Hastham Star. She has delivered more girl babies.

Example: 3

		Rahu	
	Birth		Ascendant Venus
Mars	Example 3		
	Ketu		

In the above example, Mars is exalted and posited in Sravana (Thiruvonam) star belonging to the female planet Moon. She delivered one girl baby only.

Example: 4

			Rahu
	Birth		Ascendant
	Example 4		
Ketu Jupiter			Mars (Hastham)

The fifth house from Cancer ascendant Scorpio is a female Sign owned by Mars who is posited in Virgo another female Sign and in female Star Hastham. She delivered Mrs. Indira Gandhi.

75

CHILDREN AND FORTUNE

The Four Signs Gemini, Leo, Sagittarius, and Aquarius give rise to troublesome children or the children could not be grown up satisfactorily.

For Leo Sign, 5th lord Jupiter becomes lord of 8th house too. Hence Jupiter gives mixed fortune to Leo Sign.

For Sagittarius Sign, Mars is the lord of the 5th and 12th as well giving both good and bad results.

For Gemini Sign/Rasi, Venus is the lord of the 5th and 12th extending both good and bad fortunes.

For Aquarius Sign/Rasi, Mercury is the lord of the 5th and 8th giving both and bad results.

Distress and Sorrow to Father at the time of birth of the child

The natal (birth) chart of those born when their father is in deep distress/trouble will have planetary alignments as under...

1. 9th lord will be connected to the lord of the evil.

2. Positioning of Rahu, Ketu, Saturn in trines to the Sun and the 9th house.

3. Positioning of Rahu, Ketu, and Saturn in trines to the Sun and to the lord of the 9th house.

The above planetary alignments indicate distress to the father of the child.

Scorpio Sign is indicative of stress and strain to the father in general.

Example: 1

<table>
<tr><td></td><td></td><td></td><td>Father
9th house</td></tr>
<tr><td rowspan="2">Ketu</td><td rowspan="2">Sufferings
To
Father
When
Child is born</td><td></td><td></td></tr>
<tr><td></td><td>Inimical
Rahu</td></tr>
<tr><td>Sun
Mercury</td><td></td><td>Ascendant</td><td></td></tr>
</table>

As per Libra ascendant, 9th house is Gemini whose lord is Mercury along with the Karaka for father Sun is posited in the 9th house to Kalapurusha (Time Personified) Sagittarius. For Movable Libra ascendant, the lord of the evil is 11th house lord, the Sun in this case is in Sagittarius along with Mercury, the lord of Gemini in its evil 7th house. When this child was born, there was severe poverty in the house and when they are recovered the father was not alive. The reason for the father's poverty was the planetary combination of the Sun and Mercury in trines to Rahu.

Example: 2

It can be termed right to say that the child is born when the father was at a time of distress. He could not bring up the child properly. He has to leave the native to make a earning and has to face untold miseries.

<table>
<tr><td></td><td></td><td></td><td>Ketu</td></tr>
<tr><td></td><td rowspan="2">Birth</td><td></td><td></td></tr>
<tr><td></td><td>Ascendant</td></tr>
<tr><td>Rahu

Sun</td><td></td><td></td><td></td></tr>
</table>

The evil place for fixed sign Leo ascendant the 9th house is Aries which aggravated the distress.

This child got hurt in its 7th year of age in head and left unattended without proper care. That developed into a serious disease leading to the coma stage of the child to be in the hospital for more than a year now.

The problem started the day when Ketu entered the Sagittarius Sign where conjoined Rahu and Sun was posited.

When Rahu and the Sun is combined together, any head injuries should be seriously treated with care as the Sun represents head and parts around the head.

Example: 3

			Rahu Sun
	Husband		
	Birth		Ascendant
Ketu			

The properties of the father were being sold for the treatment of the child and the sufferings of the child bothered the father much.

Distress/Sorrow/blemish through Children/in having children.

In the couple's chart, same inimical planets should not be present in the 5th house of the ascendant.

Example: 1

		Ascendant			Ascendant		
	Birth				Birth		
	Male				Female		Saturn
	Saturn						

Saturn in the male's natal (birth) chart is posited in Swati and Saturn in the female's natal (birth) chart is in Makam star. Saturn in both charts is in the stars of both Rahu and

Ketu pushing the couples together to face the blemish/ distress through/in having children.

Such blemishes are severe. As both husband and wife have to face and feel the pain of the blemish together and it is advisable not to match such natal (birth) charts during marriage.

Example: 2

In the below given charts of a couple, for one Saturn is in the 5th house and for the other Rahu is in the 5th house. As both are inimical to each other, their Bhavaga results will be very severe.

	Ketu		Ascendant
	Birth		
	Male		
		Rahu	

			Ascendant
	Birth		
	Female		
		Saturn	

Rahu in Male's chart is posited in the Chitta star in Libra and Saturn in Female's chart is in same Chitta star in Libra. As both the planets posited in the 5th house in the same star of Mars, they had to face the blemish/problems through children simultaneously.

As the couples remained childless, they have taken all possible medical care and went even to the extent of losing their lives.

SIMPLE REMEDIES TO OVERCOME THE BLEMISH THROUGH CHILDREN

When the Sun is posited in the 5th house or Leo becomes the 5th house:

Prayers to the Sun God or 'Surya Namaskar' is the best remedy.

Wheat products can be gifted to the poor. Prayers to Lamps, lights, Jyoti darshan, maintenance of street lights etc., are some remedial measures.

When the Moon is posited in the 5th house or Cancer becomes the 5th house:

Green feed, lettuce, and fodders can be gifted/fed to Cows and Goats. 'Surya Narayana' God, 'Full Moon' can be worshipped.

When Mars is posited in the 5th house or Aries/Scorpio becomes the 5th house:

If Mars is placed in the 5th house of the parent's natal (birth) chart, products made of Toor Dall mixed rice as PRASAD/ SACRAMENT in the temple for more people to eat.

It can also be given to 'Old Age Homes' and good food can be arranged for them.

Toor Dall can be donated to Lord Muruga or Durga temples to be used in oblation/sacrament. When Tamil Nadu's former Chief Minister took to ill, Toor Dall was donated to Sri

Vaitheeswaran temple. If not as a remedial measure to get rid of blemish through/in having children, donating Toor Dall helps to get relief as it is one of the Karakathuvas of Mars.

When Mercury is posited in the 5ᵗʰ house or Gemini/Virgobecomes the 5ᵗʰ house

If Mercury is placed in the 5ᵗʰ house of the Parent's natal (birth) chart, the 'Veda Mantras' pertaining to the 5ᵗʰ lord can be properly recited continuously to get rid of the blemish through Mercury posited in the 5ᵗʰ Bhavaga..

When Jupiter is posited in the 5ᵗʰ house or Sagittarius/Pisces becomes the 5ᵗʰ house

If Jupiter is placed in the 5ᵗʰ house of the Parent's natal (birth) chart, it is important to nurse and maintain elders of the family. Play toys and useful materials for children can be given to balwadis.

Giving away or donating old clothes as gift will not reduce/remove the blemish but will be a good fortune only. Only provision of eatables, food and good meals will reduce the blemish through/in having children.

When Venus is posited in the 5ᵗʰ house or Taurus/Libra becomes the 5ᵗʰ house

If Venus is placed in the 5ᵗʰ house, then donation of milk, giving away free food in temples, donation/gift of silver articles will reduce/remove the blemish.

When there exists the blemish of Venus in a natal (birth) chart of a female native, gifting silver articles required by the maternal uncles of that girl will remove the blemish to maternal uncles. The blemish of the native will also be removed.

When Saturn is placed in the 5ᵗʰ house or Capricorn/Aquarius becomes the 5ᵗʰ house

If Saturn is placed in the 5ᵗʰ house of the Parent's natal (birth) chart, donation or gift to the possible might to the poor or disabled/differently abled/defective health children will greatly erase the blemish through/in having children.

Any possible help in educating physically challenged children, maintenance of dilapidated temples, renovation of temples, renovating and reincarnating disintegrated structures and statues, maintenance and gifts, donations to old age homes, getting metal and iron utensils will do good in reducing/removing the blemish through/in having progeny/children.

When Rahu is posited in the 5ᵗʰ house

If Rahu is posited in the 5ᵗʰ house of the Parent's natal chart, kindly avoid lying to others.

Raw rice powder can be sprinkled in ant hives. Ants and termite hives can be fed with their food. Please do not mentally or physically hurt others. This is the finest remedy.

When Ketu is posited in the 5ᵗʰ house

If Ketu is posited in the 5ᵗʰ house of the Parent's natal (birth) chart, donation of gingelly oil, ghee, pooja materials to temples will relieve the blemish/curses caused in having children or problems through them due to Ketu's presence. Even donation of black clothes will be a good remedy.

PUTHRA KAMESHTI YAGAM is a good remedy. Those who are financially capable may do this yagna. This was done by King Dasharatha to have good inheritance/children through which God Sri Ramachandra Moorthy born.

77

PROGENY RESEARCH AND PRACTICE GUIDE

1. Name of the native;

2. Date of Birth/Time:

3. Place of Birth:

4. Birth Thithi/Zero/cypher(vacuum) thithi Signs:

5. Waning/Waxing Moon:

6. Bhavagas under Zero/cypher(vacuum)thithi:

7. Chethra Sputa:

8. Santhana Sputa:

9. Santhana Sun:

10. Santhana Moon:

11. Yama Sputa:

12. Santhana thithi:

13. Santhana position in degrees:

14. Jupiter's position:

15. Position of lord of the 5th:

16. Position of the 5th house:

17. Planets in the 5th house:

18. Maha Dasa (Dasa)

19. AntharDasa(Bukthi):

20. Chethra points in degrees:

21. Navamsa position:

22. Sun + Saturn:

23. Moon + Rahu:

24. Sun + Venus:

25. Jupiter + Rahu:

26. Effects of Joint horoscopes:

27. Adoption points in degrees:

STRENGTH OF THE BHAVAGA

1. When there are no Planets in a Bhavaga, the Bhavaga lord is powerful.

    If there is a planet in the Bhavaga, the planet posited in the Bhavaga is more powerful than the Bhavaga lord himself.

    This is termed as a rule reading 'the planet in the bhavaga is more powerful than the bhavaga'

2. The Bhavaga lord is powerful.

3. The Planet conjoined/combined/associated with the Bhavaga lord is powerful.

Example:

Aries ascendant, Sun + Mercury in the 4th house, Venus in the 5th house

1. For Aries ascendant, lord of the 2nd house Venus in 5th house is an Excellent strength.

    Venus Maha Dasa (Dasa) – I

2. 5th lord the Sun has second stage strength. The Sun Maha Dasa (Dasa), Anthar Dasa (Bukthi) – 2

3. Mercury associated with the Sun – Type 3 strength. Mercury – 3

    If we assume, the Bhava lord as a hotel, then

The Maha Dasa (Dasa) lord is   - the owner

The Anthar Dasa (Dasa)lord is   - the Cook

The Prithyanthar Dasa (Anthram) lord is   - the server/ supplier

The Maha Dasa (Dasa) lord is powerful here.

INDIVIDUAL STRENGTH OF THE SPERM

Male/Beejam (Seed) – The Sun, Venus, Jupiter

Female/Chethram (earth) – The Moon, Mars, Jupiter

Beejam

The sum of the positions of the Sun + Venus + Jupiter in degrees is called the Beejam. If this Beejam position in degrees falls in

1. Male Sign, Male Amsa (Navamsa) – A perfect Male to have good progeny/inheritance

2. Male Sign. Female Amsa (Navamsa) – Progeny/ childbirth after medical treatment

3. Female Sign, Male Amsa (Navamsa) or Both Sign and Amsa(Navamsa) – Weak Vigour and vitality to beget children

Such people can have children through test tubes (methods like IVF) in an artificial way. Hence medical examination before marriage is suggested in deciding the factor about begetting children.

Chethram

The sum of the positions of the Moon + Mars + Jupiter in degrees is called the Chethram. If the Chethram position in degrees falls in

1. Female Sign, Female Amsa (Navamsa) – A perfect woman capable of bearing children.

2. Female Sign, Male Amsa or Male Sign,Female Amsa (Navamsa) – Progeny/child birth after medical treatment.

3. Male Sign, Male Amsa (Navamsa) -the both in Male structure shows that the woman is barren in nature. The best way for this lady is to go for test tube baby. Complete medical examination before marriageis suggested.

Example:

To Know the Beejam – (The Sun + Venus + Jupiter)

The Sun = 216°

Venus   = 268°

Jupiter = 304°

Sum of the three 216+268+304=788-720(2 cycles of 360°) = 68degrees. This falls on Aridra 1st part (Thiruvadhirai 1 part) indicating Gemini Sign/Sagittarius Navamsa. It is in Male Sign/Male Navamsa giving the Beejam as perfect.

To know the Chethram- (The Moon + Mars+ Jupiter)

The Moon = 108°

Mars   = 158°

Jupiter   = 304°

Sum of the three 108 + 158 + 304 = 570 – 360(one cycle of 360°) =210°.Thisfallsin Visakam 3rd Part indicating Libra Sign/Gemini Navamsa. As this is Male Sign/Male Navamsa, natural inheritance of child is forbidden.

Zero/Cypher (Vacuum) thithi

Zero/Cypher (Vacuum) Thithi planet - Will not attract cosmic energy

Doing penance - Will give no results

Zero/Cypher (Vacuum) Thithi - Prevents/stops cosmic energy

The planet posited in the Zero/Cypher (Vacuum) thithi does not receive the cosmic energy.

Basedon the thithi in which a person is born, he becomes weak from 2 to 4 Signs in which thithi he is born.

Thithi Soonyam (Vacuum)- Zero/Cypher effect prevents progeny the native due to get.

The consortium of the Cosmic energy and earth energy prevents begetting children/progeny.

It gives an unsatisfactory/dejected life.

When transit Jupiter passes over the natal Mars/natal Venus under Zero/Cypher (Vacuum) Thithi, forces premature delivery or children to be born in disabled/physically challenged stage.

A healthy Beeja sputum with Zero/Cypher (Vacuum) Thithi having 5th lord will give an unwanted child.

The aspect of Jupiter on Zero/Cypher Signs will only pacify and keep it under control but will not prevent the crime and will try to hide it.

In case of joint horoscopes, if a powerful planet in a natal chart is weakened in the Zero/Cypher Sign in another horoscope, it will not permit auspicious events. Hence during the Maha Dasa (Dasa), Anthar Dasa (Bukthi) period of the planet in the Zero/Cypher Thithi Sign, the ancestors and the family (tutelary)God should be worshipped.

Monthly Zero/Cypher Day (Heriditory Results):

For those born in Chaturdasi, their month of birth where the Sun Sign is present becomes the Zero/Cypher (Vacuum) effective month. Events conducted during the course of that sign go against their clan and affect the heredity.

For those born in Chathurthi thithi, Taurus and Aquarius are the Zero/Cypher signs. Purchase of landed properties during this month will not see any growth or further expansion.

Month of Birth, Day of Birth, Star of Birth are not auspicious to start any good deeds.

1. For IVF or test tube baby treatment, transit Rahu should pass over natal Jupiter or transit Jupiter should pass over natal Rahu.

2. Transit Rahu should pass over natal Moon or the transit Moon should move over natal Rahu.

Mars and Venus are responsible for secretion of hormones and are mainly responsible for all major chemical reactions. Mars or Venus as star lord or Sign lord makes the native to look obese.

Jupiter in Mrithyu point during the birth of a child

Disability, Chronic diseases, hostility against the hereditary principles or change of sex (child becoming a eunuch).

Notes:

Three children transformed as human bombs when natal Jupiter was in 22 degrees in Cancer in their natal chart but changed their mind when transit Jupiter crossed 22 degrees.

MANUAL FOR CHILD BIRTH

Husband: Date of Birth: Time: a.m/p.m Place of Birth:

Wife: Date of Birth   Time: a.m./p.m Place of Birth:

Sl. No	Day/ Planets	Aspect of Planets/Husband	Aspect of Planets/Wife	Zero/Cypher Thithi(Sonyam)
1	Ascendant			
2	Sun			
3	Moon			
4	Mars			
5	Mercury			
6	Jupiter			
7	Venus			
8	Saturn			
9	Rahu			
10	Ketu			
11	Manti			

Bhavaga for Children and the Planets posited in it

2nd Bhavaga

5th Bhavaga

11th Bhavaga

Maha Dasa MD Anthar Dasa AD Prithyanthar Dasa PAD	As per Male Chart	Good Or Bad	As per Female Chart	Good Or Bad
2nd Bhava MD				
2nd Bhava AD				
2nd Bhava PAD				
5th Bhava MD				
5th Bhava AD				
5th Bhava PAD				
11th Bhava MD				
11th Bhava AD				
11th Bhava PAD				

Status of Jupiter:

Status of the Sun:

Status of the Moon:

Status of the 5th Lord:

Vigour/Vitality:

Beejam for Male/Husband:

Sun: Venus: Jupiter:

Should be Male Sign, Male Amsa (Navamsa)

Chethram for Female/Wife:

Moon: Mars: Jupiter:

Should be FemaleSign,Female Amsa(Navamsa)

Relativity/Connection between transit Moon with the natal (birth) chart Planets:

Planets:

Bhavagas:

As per Male natal (birth) chart:

Planet for Soul (Jeeva):   Planet for Body (Sharir):

As per Female natal (birth) chart:

Planet for Soul (Jeeva):   Planet for Body (Sharir):

Planets in Scorpion Sign:

Planets in 8th house:

Analysis of Saptamsa Varga Chakra (D7 Chart):

Navamsa Status:

Sun + Saturn:

Moon + Rahu:

Sun + Venus:

Jupiter + Rahu:

Effects as per Joint Horoscope:

Adoption points in degrees:

END

GOOD

In the Service of God

GK

9 7 9 8 8 9 4 1 5 0 0 4 8